Requiem Healing

Requiem Healing

A Christian Understanding of the Dead

MICHAEL MITTON

AND

RUSS PARKER

Foreword by Adrian Plass

daybreak
London

First published in 1991 by
Daybreak
Darton, Longman and Todd Ltd
89 Lillie Road, London SW6 1UD

Reprinted 1992

British Library Cataloguing in Publication Data
Mitton, Michael
    Requiem healing.
    1. Christianity. Doctrines. Death
    I. Title   II. Parker, Russ
    236.1

ISBN 0–232–51885–8

Unless otherwise stated
the scriptural quotations are taken from
the New International Version of the Bible
published by Hodder and Stoughton Ltd.

Phototypeset by Input Typesetting Ltd,
London SW19 8DR
Printed and bound in Great Britain by
Page Bros, Norwich

We would like to dedicate this book
to Sarah and Paul,
and to Stanley and Turve,
who pray for us

Contents

Foreword

The Protestant Church has thrown out far too many healthy babies in its panic-stricken fear of being polluted by dirty bath water. We have suffered loss and deprivation as a result.

Negative, knee-jerk responses to Mary, the mother of Jesus, have left us with an impoverished appreciation of the female elements of divinity, and an unattractively disrespectful attitude to a very special and heroic lady.

Confession is another example. Terrified of 'being incarcerated in a box with a man who is trying to do God's job for him', we heedlessly sweep away the entirely scriptural business of confessing our sins to one another. Spiritual and psychological health can sometimes depend on this process.

Often, the baby that we discard grows up elsewhere in a distorted form. Healing goes, and Christian Science grows. Spiritual gifts are neglected, and a doctrine of 'no salvation without tongues' appears.

Death, and the whole question of communication between heaven and earth, went down the theological waste-pipe a long time ago. These issues are determinedly and consistently prevented from gurgling back to the surface, particularly by the evangelical wing of the Church. Spiritualism and absorption in the occult are the mutant and very unwelcome growths that tend to fill the vacuum thus created.

Michael Mitton and Russ Parker have rescued this particular baby, washed the dirty water away and examined it carefully and calmly. Their conclusions, responsibly related to scriptural teaching, suggest that healing and wholeness for the living and the dead, requires a new understanding and awareness from people like myself, who peep fearfully out from behind the blinds of fear and prejudice.

I know the writers of this book. Jesus is at the centre of their lives, and he is at the centre of this book too – opening doors, healing hurts and shining light into dark corners as he has always done. May God bless all he touches through these pages.

ADRIAN PLASS

Introduction

The beginnings of this book happened a number of years ago when I [Michael Mitton] was serving as a curate at St Andrew's Church, High Wycombe. It was not long after I had arrived that I went to one of our weekly clergy team meetings. High Wycombe is one parish, with many team churches, and one of the benefits of this was that clergy within that team who were of different churchmanships and backgrounds met regularly together, sharing from the riches of our different traditions. I have to admit, though, to feeling rather put out on one occasion when the subject of the dead was being discussed. One of the team vicars present, who was from an Anglo-Catholic tradition, said that he could not imagine living this life without some reference to the faithful departed, to whom he prayed and from whom, he claimed, he received daily support as they prayed for him. Not only did he affirm this, he appeared passionately to believe it, and was shocked to discover that I did not share his views!

My own background is evangelical and so this catholic comment well and truly stuck in my protestant throat. 'He is wrong, of course,' I said to myself as I mused on this on the way home. Soon after this, I found myself assisting at another of the churches in the town which had an Anglo-Catholic tradition. It was a lively, loving church with a warm and happy heart. The vicar was Fr John Hadley, who was held in great affection by his church, and whom I admired and trusted. Again, assisting at the Easter liturgy I found myself confronted with this strange doctrine to do with the dead. People seemed actually to *like* the dead, but not in a spiritualistic way; they seemed to have a very real sense of the company of believers who had died, together with them in their worship. I noticed that for these people, this was an important part of their faith.

I lived with this puzzle for some time. My main problems about this were threefold: firstly, this type of acknowledgement of the dead seemed to me inexorably to lead into some type of spiritualism. Surely, if you start talking about the dead, you will start communicating with them, and then you are on the slippery slope into spiritualism. Secondly, to start acknowledging the dead in worship takes you very quickly into worshipping the dead – after all, it cannot be denied that in some parts of the world people seem to find it easier to have a personal relationship with the saints and worship them, than to have a relationship with Jesus and worship him. Then, thirdly, I could not see how you could pray for the dead without considerably diluting the gospel of salvation by faith alone. Surely, once you start praying for the dead, you are praying for them to get through purgatory to heaven, thereby 'assisting' Jesus with the work of salvation.

I imagine these are objections that many of us who come from an evangelical starting place in our pilgrimage would face. But somehow in my experience I could not just close the book and rest at ease. I was troubled in mind and spirit about this.

The more I thought about this, the more my theology seemed inadequate. It failed to come to my rescue at some important moments in my pastoral work. I remember going on a routine funeral visit and found that the bereaved family had asked for the coffin, containing the deceased mother, to be in the house for twenty-four hours prior to the funeral. So here I was doing my funeral visit, and 'Mum' was very much with us, resting in peace by the window. The mourning husband rather meekly asked, 'Would you say some prayers for her?' and we moved round the coffin and all looked on the waxen grey face of the woman who had meant so much to this family. They still loved her, just as Mary loved Jesus and wanted to show her love and respect by visiting the tomb. This woman was not a churchgoer, but she may have had faith. I did not know her final destination. I could not pray for her salvation, but I found I could pray a prayer entrusting her to God and expressing our love and sorrow to our Father in heaven. Something felt pastorally right about this and it was not inconsistent with my doctrinal objections outlined above. I remember another occasion praying with an elderly lady who was the mother of our churchwarden. She had not had a happy life, but on her deathbed she made her peace with God. I was with her and her daughter moments after she had died, and this was one of those sacred moments, that time just after a death, where you know they have gone, and yet you feel rather like someone on a railway station where you watch the train slowly disappear into the distance. Our prayer here was a sort of waving goodbye, praying for God to welcome her and to embrace her and heal her from all life's wounds. Of course, we knew he would do this anyway, but we wanted to bless what he was going to do, and, as any children, we wanted to be sure he knew what we wanted.

During this time, I came across Dr Kenneth McAll's book, *Healing the Family Tree*.[1] Here was a man who identified with no particular wing of the Church: he was pentecostal in some of his beliefs and catholic in others. The book caused me to think further about the whole area of the activity of the dead, and from this searching emerged my booklet *The Quick and the Dead*.[2] I was helped in the writing of that booklet by Russ Parker, and as we talked and discussed the subject together it seemed right to us to put our thoughts down in the form of this book.

This book, then, is by both of us. We have each taken separate chapters and you will see initials by each chapter heading in the Contents to tell you who has written it.

Russ now writes about how he has been drawn into this area:

In the autumn of 1975 a number of threads came together in my life which resulted in a new perspective on the issue of healing past hurts, especially when they related to an unplanned and painful death or unfinished bereavement. Before this time I had not properly considered the appropriateness or otherwise of remembering the dead or as to how the living might be still affected by their dead relatives. As an evangelical the dead were a closed book; they were either saints in glory or those awaiting judgement. In either case, their situation was known only to God and there was to be no tampering in this area and no changes to be expected now that they were dead. As Christians, the only constructive response to make was thanksgiving and praise to God for those whose faith had enabled them to be taken home to be forever with their heavenly father. Those who delved any further into this subject were either spiritualists or Roman Catholics. However, I was to gain some fresh insights into this whole area and in the process discover something more of the healing ministry of the Lord Jesus Christ. The journey, like so many, began with personal pain.

The story properly begins in the winter of 1972 when my wife Carole had a miscarriage when she lay in bed one night. By the time the doctor arrived the event was almost over. I was hurriedly removed from the room and later told that the foetus had been rejected and that it was just as well as it was hopelessly malformed. I can remember quite distinctly the way he told me this in cool, casual and clinical tones as he walked through the flat and made for the door. He was precise and practical and told me to make sure that my wife rested for a few days, after which she could get up and life would return to normal. All the while he was talking I wanted to stop him using the term 'foetus', because it felt so impersonal. It felt to me as if a real life was being depersonalised. I felt angry and

I wanted to shout at him but at the same time I felt foolish about my feelings.

Carole and I felt numb about the incident for a time and then drifted back into circulation together. Yet we both were aware of some unfinished business in our hearts which every now and again would surface and we would feel the sense of loss for the child who never was. The following years were spent in pioneer evangelism on a council estate in the suburbs of Birkenhead. These were tough and, quite often, depressing days. By now we had two healthy children but, shortly after the birth of our son, Carole was severely ill with post-natal depression. I was made redundant. It was during this time that we lost another child in a similar way to the first. And, like that earlier time, we tried to put it all to one side, but it was much more difficult the second time. There followed another two years of unemployment during which time the Church at which we worked was closed down. This was like another death and it filled us with depression, and to a great degree linked in with the feelings of loss for our two other children who might have been. Yet Carole and I did not really share how we felt about what had happened. We buried it inside ourselves, but every now and again my feelings of guilt and sadness would surface. As I had no one to talk to, the matter remained there.

In 1975 I was invited to speak at Foxhills, the Anglican diocesan centre for the Chester diocese. My brief was to give some talks on the basic principles of counselling and healing. I learned that the other speaker was to be Dr Kenneth R. McAll. When I was told that he was a psychiatrist and a G.P. among many other things, I felt anxious that I would not match up to his level of ministry. It was through Ken's talks that I was to come face to face with my unfinished bereavement. To some degree his talks focused upon the counselling he had given to parents who had lost children through miscarriage or abortion. Immediately my repressed feelings were aroused and

I felt as if my own inner hurt was being coaxed up into the open. When dealing with clients who were suffering either from depression or anxiety and for which no apparent reason could be found, Ken would ask his patients if there had been other problems in the family's experience. Quite often this form of enquiry would go so far as to include children who had been aborted or lost through a miscarriage. (On other occasions the problem was seen to relate to adults who had died without being prepared or who, in death, still carried unresolved burdens with them.) Quite a lot said that they had, and some would share their initial regret regarding the experience but there, they had thought, the matter ended. Ken would then ask the parents if they had held a proper funeral service for their lost child and then named him or her in faith before God. The usual response was one of surprise for most of the parents had discounted the foetus as a real person. However, Ken shared that in almost every case when they re-owned their lost child and prayed for him and named him before the Lord, and even apologised for not owning him as a real child, the illness or trauma was healed.

Dr McAll maintained that what in effect had been happening was that the young children, in being rejected or ignored, had tried to signal their presence to living members of the family. Usually they chose someone who would be more receptive to them and such people would in fact begin to feel the emotions of the dead child – feelings such as rejection, depression and a sense of lostness. He gave as an example the story of a young boy who, totally out of character, began to steal things from the local shops. He was a normal child who enjoyed the love and security of his home. Indeed, he gave away all the things he stole as he had no need for them. Neither was he suffering from any kind of pressure. Therefore his mother took him to the school counsellor and to various consultants in an effort to understand his behaviour: all to no avail. Eventually his mother came and shared her concern with Ken. In his usual manner he drew up a chart listing all the members of the family and then asked if there were any members who were now deceased. The answer was a partial no. When Ken asked for clarification the lady said that some years before her son was born she had had an abortion. This child was duly prayed for and named in faith and the mother apologised for what she had done. From that day onwards her son ceased to steal from the shops!

As I listened to this and other case-histories of healings, I was making a number of theological objections. Surely there is to be no contact between the living and the dead; did not the parable of the rich man and Lazarus make this clear? (Luke 16:19–31). Ken was implying that the dead affect the health of the living. Was he confusing the fact of demonic oppression with his ideas of people being stuck in a sort of limbo state? And might not this way of thinking lead those who are sick to project their problems onto the dead and not take responsibility for their own lives. Another objection was that of universalism. If the living, by recognising the dead, can set them free from being trapped, then surely this implies a better salvation potential than personal commitment to Jesus Christ as Lord and Saviour. It seemed that anybody recognised by the living, irrespective of their relationship to Jesus, could now enter heaven. As an evangelical I found I was objecting to what I was hearing.

However, in my heart I simply started to cry. Whatever questions I was raising in my mind, I suddenly realised that the two children lost years earlier through miscarriage were real human beings. I had been trying to push them out of my mind and accept that they were nothing of value. Ken's talks had helped me to understand that no matter how physically incomplete they were, they were made in the image of God just as much as I had been. This meant for me, suddenly and wonderfully, that we had another two children. They had been lost to us but never to God. It occurred to me that they had gone straight to be with the Lord and had in fact been growing up in heaven with their Father, the saints and the angels! My immediate response was to get alone and pray about this. I went to my room as soon as I could, and in the presence of God I recognised our two children and gave thanks to God for them and said that I would be looking forward to meeting them when I go home to be with my heavenly Father. I also said to God that I was sorry for not recognising them as being real people and belonging to our family. I felt a deep peace inside and the pain and depression which had daunted me for a number of years was gone. Also I felt a sense of being a complete father. It may sound absurd, but there is no other way to describe how it felt. I went home and told Carole what I had done. Far from regarding my actions as foolish or heretical she felt that she had been excluded from something that deeply affected her also. For a while this separated us but eventually we both came to the place of recognising and accepting our two lost lives. Carole felt a deep warm glow inside and was aware of a sense of wholeness not known before.

In reflecting on all of this I can say that I have experienced a real inner healing. Yet as a conservative evangelical have I suddenly stepped on to a bypath meadow?

Russ ends up asking the same question as I do. It came to me when I was discussing the question of journeys at a conference I was attending. I remember talking about this part of the journey and how it was for me as an evangelical. I said that it felt for me as if I was exploring a country road and came across an interesting area of woodland that I wanted to explore. The woodland represented the whole area that this book is discussing, which is to do with a Christian understanding of the dead. However, around this wood there was a substantial fence, and by this fence was placed a sign which read:

WARNING!
NO EVANGELICALS ALLOWED IN HERE.
PROMINENT LEADERS HAVE EXPLORED
THIS AREA AND FOUND IT TO BE
DANGEROUS!
GO NO FURTHER!

and the awkward part of me wanted to know why I could not go further. And if it really is forbidden territory then I want to know why.

So as we now get into the book we invite you to explore with us. It is our conviction that, far from being a hostile and forbidden world, this woodland can offer some surprising treasure which will enrich our understanding of life and death, and will affect the way we pastor the bereaved, foster hope in the faithful, commit the dead to God and deliver the oppressed.

All Souls 1990   MICHAEL MITTON
                                                  RUSS PARKER

1

Feelings for the Dead

When Pope John XXIII was told that he was going to die he remarked, 'My bags are packed, I am ready to leave!'

BEREAVEMENT AND LOSS

Death is a subject which is not usually a part of our everyday conversation, but for a time towards the end of the 1980s it was seldom out of the newspaper headlines. In those closing years of the decade there seemed to be an unprecedented number of tragic accidents which took the lives of many hundreds of people. In one sixteen-month period between March 1987 and July 1988 three, possibly preventable, accidents claimed the lives of 391 people. Millions watched intently as television newsreels showed the sad pictures of the sinking of the passenger ferryboat 'Herald of Free Enterprise' when it tipped on its side and went down in the English Channel just outside Zeebrugge with the loss of 193 lives. The other two disasters in question were the fire at Kings Cross station in London in November 1987, where thirty-one people perished in the flames, and the explosion of the Piper Alpha platform in the North Sea claiming the lives of 167 men, many of whom have never been found so that they could be properly buried.

For many there are graphic scenes of such tragedies firmly imprinted upon their minds. Who can forget the sight of the crowds running for their lives from the burning stands of the

Bradford City football ground, or of the policeman there with his hair on fire, still trying to rescue others? Gail Cook was one of the survivors of the Zeebrugge ferry and in an interview she said:

> I still don't sleep properly. It all still runs through my mind and even when I do sleep I'm dreaming about it . . . I dreamed of my friend on there the other night. He kept saying to me, 'I'm not dead, I'm still with you.'[1]

As the nation began to adjust to life after the oil rig disaster there was another series of appalling accidents within six months. The issue of death once again became immediate to the populace. Just before Christmas 1988 a Pan Am 747 jet was blown out of the sky by a terrorist bomb, killing all 270 passengers. The shattered plane scattered its debris over the Scottish town of Lockerbie, killing yet more people. The Prime Minister as well as other dignitaries, including the Prince of Wales, visited the site of the crash. In the same month there was a serious train collision at Clapham where thirty-three people died in the wreckage. Then, as soon as the Christmas celebrations were over, a British Midland plane crash-landed on the M1 motorway near Kegworth in Derbyshire, claiming the lives of forty-six people. I remember how deeply it affected many of the local clergymen who were called to pray with the dying and the dead. One in particular described how painful he found it to be in the fuselage of the broken aircraft amongst many who were crying and calling out for comfort. 'It was like being in a communal grave,' he said. As if this were not enough tragedy to contemplate, in the following April ninety-five Liverpool football fans were crushed to death whilst watching their team play in a semi-final game at the Hillsborough ground in Sheffield. Seemingly the final act in this spate of death was that of the Thames pleasure boat which was rammed one September night and sank very quickly with the loss of twenty-nine young lives.

The nation seemed to be reeling from one shock after another. The public outrage at such loss of life led to heated debates in the Houses of Parliament and more than likely provoked the dismissal of the Transport Minister of the day, Mr Paul Channon. The government was forced to take another look at its safety measures for public transportation. For the City of Liverpool, with the loss of so many of its people, there seemed to be a sense of national mourning. For a few weeks after the event, whilst the continuation of the FA Cup matches hung in the balance, thousands of people visited the home ground at Anfield and laid almost a quarter of a million wreaths on the pitch. Young and old alike paraded in silence into the ground to offer their own token of respect; many wept quite openly. The scenes seemed more reminiscent of an Armistice Day parade than football fans grieving the loss of friends.

Such mourning I am sure is quite real, but, except for the relatives and friends of those who died, it is largely grieving from a distance. It soon passes as people return to their routines of life. However, when the death is personal, the process of bereavement is not so easily dismissed. I remember inviting a retired GP to give a series of talks at a Christian counselling course on the subject of bereavement. As she spoke she suddenly stopped and began to cry; she very quickly stopped herself and apologised, saying that she still missed her husband enormously. He had died over ten years earlier. Her candour actually helped others to begin sharing some of their own unfinished grieving and it became a valuable time of learning for all concerned. The sense of loss can be very powerful and does affect people in different ways.

The term 'bereavement' comes from the word 'reave' which means 'to ravage, rob and leave desolate'. It is no small wonder then that the grieving person can feel depressed, anxious, hostile and hysterical. There may be frequent bouts of physical pain and total weakness. Others may feel numb or find difficulty sleeping or controlling their bowel movements. Sometimes the feelings of grief are locked inside until something happens to us which triggers the feelings and there is a bursting out of grief in tears and cries. This is quite beneficial for it is rather as if an underground stream, having been blocked by a fallen rock, is now free of its obstruction and can flow normally. It is important to say now that grieving is a normal and healthy process which must not be hurried through. At the end of this journey there is to be healing, a coming to terms with loss and life and so going on into the future. For the Christian we must take to heart that it is those who do actually mourn whom Christ will bless and comfort (Matt. 5:4). It is precisely for these reasons that a period of ritual mourning is important; it helps to underline that there has been a loss and that there has to be a going on from this point. John Hinton makes this point very well when he says:

> The practice of mourning provides more than this socially approved catharsis of grief. It insists that the death has occurred, repeatedly demonstrating this fact over a few days so that the bereaved, whatever their state of mind, accept the painful knowledge, assimilate it and begin to plan accordingly. Viewing the body and taking part in the funeral emphasises beyond all doubt that the person is really dead. The condolences, the discussion of the deceased in the past tense, the newspaper announcements, the public recognition of the death, all affirm the loss.[2]

However, there are many people today who get stuck in their grieving, who cannot or will not make the mourner's journey to wholeness. Consider, for example, the stark contrast in response to the death of a son in the lives of the Ayatollah Khomeini and 'Daddy' King, the father of Martin Luther King Jr. The Ayatollah's hatred for the Shah of Iran and for his American supporters began when his son was executed by the Shah. From his unresolved grief came the desire for revenge which eventually caused an international crisis and entangled the whole Middle East in a conflict which is still unresolved. Daddy King's grief for his son took a different route and led to peace rather than war. After Martin Luther King was murdered the King family gathered together and resolved that Martin's vision of peace would die with him unless they forgave the murderer. Together they grieved for Martin; they cried until they came to the place where they could pray and forgive. Because of their process of grieving they were enabled to move forward in their lives and carry on their commitment to non-violent service to freedom.

Elisabeth Kübler-Ross, in her book *On Death and Dying*,[3] says that the first identifiable response to the subject of death is denial. The individual pushes the subject of death away because it is too threatening and disturbing. In an attempt to maintain balance in life, the one who is dying or grieving a loss, denies that there is a death to be faced or overcome. In time the denial moves through the process of anger, bargaining, depression and then finally acceptance. Another way of summarising this procedure is to say that mourning helps us to move from still holding on to the dead to letting go of the dead. We shall now explore some of the reasons why people hold on to their dead.

HOLDING ON TO THE DEAD

For many the adjustment to accepting the finality of death and separation takes time. Consequently there are many examples of the bereaved sensing the dead as still 'being there' with them. This may go as far as feeling the loved one's arm around them, hearing their voice speaking comforting words or giving guidance. Others report smelling the tobacco of his familiar pipe or seeing her walking down the street or sitting in a favourite armchair. It must be stated that for many this brings great comfort, and as Christians we must be sensitive not to demolish such feelings in our haste to be theologically accurate and defensive. The most common explanation is that the bereavement is so intolerable that the unconscious mind refuses to believe that a death has happened, and so manufactures this kind of phenomenon in an attempt to convince the conscious mind that the loved one is still alive and present. Counsellors can usually help the bereaved person to come to terms with the death and so let go.

Another reason why some people hold on to their dead is because they believe that they are silent companions or guides for the living. Alan Billings points out the folk culture in a lot of people's understanding of death when he quotes the following from the obituary columns of the *Leicester Mercury*:

> Those we love don't go away
> They walk beside us every day
> Unseen, unheard, but always near
> Still loved, still missed, still very dear.[4]

He goes on to say that such verses are not necessarily evidence of religious faith but examples of how religious imagery is all that is available to nominal believers for expressing their thoughts and feelings. It is here that the minister must be careful not to collude with such fantasies whilst seeking to support the hurting. The reality of death must not be denied, and so Billings encourages the Christian in pastoral care to avoid using terms such as 'falling asleep' which, though mentioned in the Bible, may dull the sharp reality of death. As Christians we are to encourage a recognition that the deceased person is now with God who is all just and loving, and in our mourning we are to come to the place where we recognise this and leave our loved ones in God's capable hands.

Another reason why people hold on to their dead is because they are told that the dead wish to hold on to them. Some years ago I was speaking to a self-help bereavement group in Leicester. One of the elderly widowers in that group came up to me and said that he had been contacted by a local Spiritualist church to say that in one of their meetings a medium had received a communication from his wife who had died some six weeks earlier. If he would care to come to one of their meetings he would hear for himself what his wife wished to say to him. This he duly did, and now he lived for the moments he could go to the meetings in the hope of hearing from his former partner. I could not help feeling angry and sad at the same time: angry because he was getting involved in something which is clearly opposed to the Christian message, namely that of trying to contact the dead (cf. Deut. 18:10–12); sad because he still seemed unhappy and, because of his frequent and often forlorn visits to the meetings, was not being allowed to go through the process of grieving which would have led him to a more wholesome approach to life and death.

We must admit and accept that there has indeed been a revival of interest in the world of psychic phenomena and spiritualism. For example, film stars such as Shirley MacLaine publicly endorses her spirit guide and Linda Evans of the Dynasty soap opera shares that she has followed guidance from a discarnate entity named Mafu. On television there have been programmes showing how certain people have tried to contact the dead, as was the case on Central Television some years ago when friends vainly tried to contact the departed life of Doris Stokes. Further interest in holding on to the dead is aroused by claims that the dead continue their life's work through the living. In a programme on BBC2 television called 'Spirits from the Past', screened on 23 October 1989, the renowned pianist John Lill claimed that the composer Beethoven was enabling him to play better by communicating part of his mind to the pianist. Such claims abound and many are being given consideration. Recently the London Symphony Orchestra, together with the Ambrose Singers, performed a sacred oratorio called 'Beyond the Veil', which was allegedly composed by Handel and communicated two years ago by the dead composer to a spiritualist teacher.

A more modernised form of this belief is provided by the so-called 'New Age movement'. The Christian Gospel proclaims that beyond the fact of death there is a resurrection life to be experienced through our Lord Jesus Christ: New Agers, however, are seemingly denying the very fact and content of death. The humanist psychologist Maxine Negri says that they believe all human goals appear possible, including breaching the dividing wall of death, not through Jesus Christ or Mohammed or other 'divine' messengers, but through one's own human, independently earned, spiritual enlightenment.[5] What is meant by this is that we have the ability to tap into the life essence or spirit of the departed and so remain in contact. It is not so clear if this also means a continuation of the relationship with the dead in a manner similar to when they were alive.

In the next chapter we shall examine much more closely what the Bible has to say about contact with the departed, but suffice it to say here that such interest in alleged contacts creates a climate of confusion as to just where are the frontiers which separate the living and the dead. The matter is made more complex by two further areas of reported contact with the dead – that of clinical or near death experiences and the healings which many claim to have received through praying for the sins and needs of departed ancestors. Dr Raymond Moody, in his book *Life After Life*,[6] wrote about the stories patients related to him when they had had near-death experiences. The dying man may have heard his doctor pronounce him dead, while at the same time he may have felt as if his body was being sucked rapidly through a long tunnel where he seemed to approach a 'being of light'. Relatives and friends who had died would come forward and help bring him towards the light. All this would be accompanied by feelings of great acceptance and warmth and a complete absence of judgement. The majority of those who return from such encounters say that they are now more

determined to live a fuller and better life and this often includes
some form of religious commitment.

A lot of research has gone into this phenomenon and, whilst
many do not give credence to the stories being actual encounters of a person who has died, they nonetheless say that it is a
healing experience. Such accounts raise a number of questions
as far as conservative evengelical belief is concerned. For example, do these stories mean that there is no accounting for
personal sin and that there is no need to repent and be born
again? Such testimonies of non-judgmentalism and acceptance
for all, irrespective of whether the person was a practising
Christian or not, surely implies a universalism where there is
no need for conversion and an embracing of the gospel of
salvation. Matthew and Dennis Linn respond to this question
by saying that people are far more likely to be motivated to
faith and Christian living by the image of a loving and forgiving
Father rather than a vindictive and judgemental father.[7] They
support their statement by referring to the Prodigal Son who
never found his restored place in the family until he received
the embrace of his accepting and loving father. Then came
confession and new life (Luke 15:20ff). However, this is an
oversimplification of the story because they overlook the fact
that the son first underwent a period of conviction and repentance before returning to his father's embrace (Luke 16:17–20).

However, I do not think that it is suitable to use these
experiences as a means to formulate beliefs about the nature
of salvation or the alleged absence of judgement. Neither do I
think that such encounters are demonic in origin because of
the implications of universalism and the absence of reference
to the unique salvation offered through Jesus Christ. What is
quite obvious is that the patients do not die but recover. Therefore, we do not have a death and a salvation without the need
of conversion. What we do have is an awareness that God, the
Supreme Being, is by nature one of love and forgiveness. This
is Good News for the fallen, and those who do recover have

gone on with a greater openness to God in their lives. This may not be salvation as we would like it, but it does give a better opportunity for the individual to respond to the Gospel at a later date. It must not be forgotten either that such people who have been resuscitated have also been confronted with their sinfulness, and Dr Maurice Rawlings, who worked for many years in the resuscitation unit of a large hospital in Chicago, describes how he prayed with one such person to be saved and who went on to live a committed Christian life.[8]

The appearance of the dead in some of the stories quoted in *Life after Life* does not suggest necessarily that such departed have been automatically saved when they were known to have lived without Christ when they were alive. After all, we are not certain if these people are actually there or are just a part of the person's unconscious thinking. So all we can state confidently on this matter at the moment is that, for the person concerned, such deceased are important to them for differing reasons and that they too are sharing the same awareness.

The traditional evangelical teaching on relationships between the living and the dead is that there is to be no contact at all. Richard Bewes says that the biblical revelation does not seem to encourage the merging of this world and the next. If we try to do this, several errors begin to raise their heads; 'sentimentalism . . . sensationalism, where discipleship can become diverted and blunted . . . and spiritualism.'[9] Yet we do believe as Christians that these two worlds will be merged at the glorious reunion of all the dead in Christ and those who will still be alive on the earth on the day when Jesus Christ will return in power and glory (1 Thess. 4:15–18). Any crossing of the boundaries between the living and the dead before this event are regarded with the deepest suspicions.

The kind of sightings we have just been discussing are therefore regarded as entirely subjective in nature, and people are advised not to dwell upon such experiences. Whilst the perspective of this book is not to encourage any seeking after the dead or involvement with spiritism, we nonetheless recognise that for many people such near-death encounters do produce a less anxious approach to death. We would also acknowledge the need in us to cherish and continue to love those who have died. This we believe does not conflict with evangelical belief. Some Christians believe that such events should be more openly accepted as part of God's providence and received as a gift to encourage us to live more positively and look to our future hope of life eternal with more determined peace of heart.

This was certainly conveyed by the story of Jean Darnell as recorded in her autobiography *Heaven Here I Come*. Jean relates how she and her mother were converted to Christ through an evangelistic mission when she was about nine years old. Not long after this time her mother had a serious illness and died. A registered nurse had been on the scene and pronounced her dead. Both Jean and her father were stunned by this sudden death. Jean cried and cried and prayed that Jesus would give her mother back to them. Whilst she was crying and praying, her mother 'came back to life'. The story that unfolded from her mother was not dissimilar to those told by Moody and Rawlings, save for the fact that Jean's mother recognised her own mother who came and escorted her to a lovely garden. She was so sure it was her mother even though she had never met her, for she had died three days after giving birth. Shortly after this Jesus called Jean's mother and said her spirit was to return to earth because her daughter was crying for her so much. What also makes this story interesting is that, at a later date, Jean's mother told her that she had visited her own mother's eldest sister, Aunt Sis, in West Virginia and was shown an old photograph of a group of people. Her mother instantly pointed out her own mother and said that this was the woman whom she had met in Heaven. Apparently this was the only photograph of Jean's grandmother, and neither Jean nor her mother had ever seen it.[10]

So near-death encounters with the dead, whilst not strictly

provable, do not really infringe upon our basic belief that we are to leave the dead in the hands of God. These are extreme examples and were not deliberately sought after, but they do suggest that there may be some area of legitimate encounter with the departed. They at least convey to us that our departed are still important to us, and this fact should not be minimised or denied.

PRAYING FOR THE DEPARTED

The second area of contact with the dead in our discussion is that of prayers for the departed, because in some way, it is alleged, they are continuing to influence the living. This does not necessarily involve the sighting of the deceased. It concerns the belief that the issues which were bound up with the deceased relatives are in some way being visited upon the living. There is certainly a great deal of evidence in the Bible that the sins of the parents can indeed be brought upon their descendants and for a number of generations. The most often quoted reference in the Bible to this phenomenon is 'I the Lord am a jealous God, punishing the children for the sin of the father to the third and fourth generation of those who hate me, but showing love to a thousand generations of those who love me and keep my commandments' (Exod. 20:5, 34:7; Num. 14:18; Deut. 5:9, to quote a few). In addition to these references are those of curses where it is written that the sins of the parents will take the effect of a curse being visited upon the children who shall come afterwards. Such generational effects will be diseases, disasters and lingering illnesses (Deut. 28:59; see also 28:18, 32; 30:1–2, 19). However, it must also be pointed out that in the opinion of some scholars the visiting of sins down through the generations has been cancelled out by the new covenant God has made by which the individual will now be accountable only for their own sins. For example,

Ezekiel questions whether the saying, 'The fathers have eaten our sour grapes and set the children's teeth on edge' is still true (Ezek. 18:2). He goes on to say that from now on the salvation of individuals will be attributed to their own choices and not that of their parents (Ezek. 18:17ff).

However, it is a matter of observation that very often the twists and scars of our parents' experiences can be carried on within the family because the children are indeed shaped by the parents' approach to life. I know in my own case that I grew up in a family where sons and fathers did not really get on well with each other. This puzzled me at first because I tried very hard to get close to my father, but with little or no success. Then some years later, as I pursued my hobby of family history, I discovered that my father hardly knew my grandfather because the latter was quite withdrawn. My grandfather in turn could not get on with his father, a policeman, because he too was a remote figure who was hardly ever at home. My great-grandfather lost his father when he was young because he had to leave home to work and soon afterwards his father died. I was able to trace a pattern of behaviour down through the fathers and sons which was fairly similar. The chain was only broken when I recognised what was happening and through prayer asked God to break the cycle in my life by giving me a real capacity to love as a father and be loved as a person. I am happy to report that, although I have not succeeded in getting a lot further with my own father, my son and I do enjoy a good relationship and like and love each other very well.

An extension of this syndrome is the belief that not only have the problematic issues of the parents been passed down to their children, but that the parents or ancestors themselves have somehow maintained a contact or hold over their offspring. In this latter case the form of ministry which is usually recommended here is a prayer recognising the deceased in question and an acceptance of their sins and needs before God. It is often carried out in the form of a communion service. This is a practice which has long been recognised in the Roman Catholic and Anglo-Catholic churches but which the evangelical Christian has rejected because it seems to undermine belief in the finality of death and judgement. Such practices seem to be offering a second chance of salvation to the deceased and so implies that the ministry of the church at prayer is more effective than that of the atoning death of Jesus upon the cross. We shall look at this very closely when we examine the work of Dr Ken McAll, the foremost practitioner of this form of healing, in a later chapter.

Perhaps the most well-known form in which this ministry is presented is that of dealing with ghosts and hauntings. Those who suffer from such appearances say that they are convinced that a real person is bothering them. On 16 January 1990 I took part in the programme 'The Time, the Place' on Central Television. Of the many who shared their stories one woman called Joy talked about waking up in her bedroom to find a man leaning over her and almost smothering her. No words were exchanged but she was convinced that this 'person' was in some way asking for help. The question of the Christian is, 'What is the appropriate response to this kind of event?' Whether we are dealing with the subjective life of the person, the demonic or the unquiet dead, we need to recognise that we are at least handling how the living feel about the dead. Therefore we must accept such feelings and be sensitive about how we proceed. We also need to recognise that in our ministry to the one in need – whether it is bereavement, a haunting of some kind, or some kind of personal attachment to the departed – we must bring them to the place where they learn to free the dead.

FREEING THE DEAD

> Dying has become a more remote part of our lives . . . when
> death occurs there is a fair chance that someone else [not a
> member of the family] will be the witness and that the care
> that precedes it will be done by others. So the language of
> death is foreign to us.[11] (Words in brackets mine.)

Before we can free those who have problems with the dead we
must enable them to come to terms with dying itself. We are
still not as comfortable with the subject of death as were our
Victorian ancestors, for whom it was an all too common event.
It was no surprise for there to be at least one or two infant
deaths in an average household. Therefore grieving, tears and
talking about the dead was a familiar feature of public and
family life. However, even in Christian circles there is still
difficulty in balancing feelings of grief with a robust belief
in resurrection and eternal life. I remember two funerals in
particular which represented for me a closed and an open
approach to grieving for the Christian. The first was upon the
occasion of the death of a college principal's wife who was
about seventy years old. As the cortège processed into the
church, the widower walked behind the coffin and although the
congregation was singing a song of triumph, he looked sad and
his face was quite pale. I overheard someone a few rows behind
me say, 'Look at him! He should be praising, not looking so
sad and unbelieving.' It seems that they could not equate pain
and sadness with hope and faith in bereavement. For them the
husband should have been triumphant and not showing or
perhaps feeling the sense of loss. How intolerant we Christians
can be when another is hurting. Even Jesus wept at a funeral
and he is the Resurrection and the Life!

The second funeral took place in Richmond Baptist Church
in Liverpool. This time it was the death of a young mother
whose husband was a minister, and the cortège entered the

church with the husband and their five-year-old daughter walking side by side. The address was given by the widower who began his talk by saying, 'I don't know why God let my wife suffer so much pain and die like she did in that car crash. I wish I did. I don't know why he let us move house only to have Ann die three months later. I don't know why.' You can imagine how emotional everyone was feeling by now. Then he went on to say, 'But I do know this, that Jesus died for us all and rose again. That Jesus has promised eternal life to all those who trust in him. And what I do know helps me to live with what I don't know.' Here was hurt and hope being given equal expression. It is this voicing of feeling and faith which brings balance into the journey of dying and which gives us a better opportunity to let go of the dying and learn to free them into God's hands. It is an inability to free the dying that leads us to hold on to them even after death. There also seems some room to conclude that the dead, because they were not properly prepared for their death, try to hold on to the living.

Whilst this is not a book about bereavement care and counsel we feel nonetheless that it is important to encourage people to approach the issue of death in as whole and caring a fashion as possible. It is this letting go at dying and death that prevents any unhealthy holding on to the dead. It will also give us a better understanding when we meet people who say that they are still in contact with those who have died. We may well discover that the continued relationship with the departed is because there is some form of unfinished business which concerned either the deceased or the living relative which has not yet been brought under the healing power of the Lord Jesus Christ.

Sheila Cassidy, in her book *Sharing the Darkness*, says of caring for the dying, that 'It is here that we must learn the spirituality of the foot of the cross, the stance of the impotent bystander.'[12] She goes on to list three basic attributes which we need in order to accompany the dying; first, an intensely down-to-earth practicality that does not flinch from the impact of the disintegration of human bodies and minds. The second is a much needed sense of humour, for life and death carries its tragi-comedy moments. Finally there is the need for a special sensitivity, a vulnerability to the pain of others that is often, but not always, the result of personal experience of suffering. It is these same qualities that are needed when we share with those who have continued a relationship with the departed. There is a need for them to go on the journey which the dying take and where the living learn to let go and free the one they love. It is not enough to sound out the dangers of spiritualism and possible deception. We need to uncover the issues that prevent the living from letting go of their dead and, in Jesus' name, direct his healing peace into their lives.

So far we have been saying that the living have all kinds of feelings about the dead and dying and which to some degree account for the way the living sustain a relationship with those who have died. This being the case, we have discussed the need for such people to be enabled to let go of their dying and dead and so enter into an appropriate relationship with their departed. Here we recognise a general failing, particularly among evangelicals, to recognise and accept any kind of relating between the living and the departed. The very fact that we treasure the memory of our loved ones in our hearts means that we are still saying to them, 'I love you and recognise your right to life.' So we now need to examine carefully if there are any relationships between the living and the dead which the Bible allows and which may be open to us, the living.

> Dear Master, all the flowers are Thine,
> And false the whisper, 'ours' and 'mine';
> We lift our hearts to Thee and say,
> 'Lord, it was Thine to take away.'
>
> And yet, though we would have it so,
> Lord, it is very good to know

That Thou art feeling our pain,
And we shall have our flower again.

So help us now to be content
To take the sorrow Thou has sent.
Dear Lord, how fair Thy house must be
With all the flowers we've lent to Thee![13]

2

Meeting with the Dead: A Biblical Survey

> Jesus has forced open a door that has been locked since the death of the first man. He has met, fought, and beaten the king of death. Everything is different because He has done so. (C. S. Lewis)

It is a basic Christian belief that God has access to the world of the living as well as the dead. Jesus underlined this truth when he said that his father was not the God of the dead but of the living (Mat. 22:32).[1] What makes this statement so startling was that Jesus had just been referring to the patriarchs, Abraham, Isaac and Jacob, who had been dead for centuries! They were obviously not dead to God but ever live before him. This also suggests quite strongly that the dead have an ongoing relationship with God. The Scriptures give us some glimpses into the nature of this relationship. In the Old Testament there are many references to the dead being like shadows of their former selves and inhabiting the world of 'Sheol'.[2]

Here they dwell in darkness and silence.[3] Great and humble alike live side by side in pale equality. Both Isaiah and Ezekiel write of God addressing the proud rulers of the nations as they come down into Sheol. We are told that even the dead are roused to speak to these men and remind them of how they have been reduced from their former glory.[4] However, this shadowy state of existence was essentially something that the dead longed to be freed from into a fuller life in the presence of God. David represents this hope when he says:

. . . You will not abandon me to the grave,
nor will you let your Holy One see decay.
You have made known to me the path of life;
you will fill me with joy in your presence,
with eternal pleasures at your right hand. (Ps. 16:10–11)[5]

When we come to the New Testament there is much more
of an indication that there is some sort of conscious awareness
for the dead in the interval between death and resurrection.
Before we look at these references we need to say something
about 'soul sleep'. In a number of places the dead are referred
to as those who sleep. Paul, when he seeks to encourage the
Thessalonian church to hold on to their belief in the resurrection and to look forward to restored relationships with the
dead, says to them: 'We do not want you to be ignorant about
those who fall asleep, or to grieve like the rest of men, who
have no hope. We believe that Jesus died and rose again and
so we believe that God will bring with Jesus those who have
fallen asleep in him (1 Thess. 4:13–14).[6]

It has largely been assumed that these references mean that
the dead have no conscious awareness of their state and only
awake at the resurrection time. However, this is both to miss
the purpose of the metaphor as well as to misunderstand the
nature of dreaming itself. The purpose of the metaphor of sleep
is to say that the individual has not ceased to exist because
they have died and been buried. For them life goes on even if
we cannot relate to them as we would to any normal waking
person. They sleep only in so far as we can perceive their state
of existence but this does not mean that for them they are not
awake to the realities of being in the eternal presence of God.
Secondly, and although this was probably not the uppermost
thought in the use of this term, sleep is now known to be
a highly active experience for the sleeper, whose mind and
awareness are in fact in constant use.

Let us now conclude this section by looking at the imagery

which suggests an ongoing and developing relationship with God for those who have died and who await their resurrection day when they shall be reunited with all the faithful in Christ. We find that many of these glimpses are given by Jesus himself in his teaching. In the fourth gospel Jesus speaks of dying in terms of going to the Father's house (John 14:2). Dr Westcott said that here we must not be misled into thinking of modern, Western style rooms, but rather that of a resting place or station on a great road where travellers found refreshment.[7] Archbishop Temple says the word used here means a wayside *caravanserai*, which was akin to a motel for the camel caravans which crossed the great areas of the ancient world. At night, when all the guests had arrived and the animals were secured, a friendly and convivial spirit prevailed. Such travellers would send on ahead a dragoman to prepare for the arrival of the caravan. So Jesus presents himself as our dragoman who has gone on ahead to prepare a resting place on the journey to the final destination.[8] Temple draws out this theme of the resting place and underlines that in this case it is not the final destination for the Christian. It is indeed a fellowship with Christ, fuller than before, but it is a stage on the journey as we press on to 'the goal of the call upward which God gives in Christ Jesus'.[9] It is quite conceivable then that the time the dead spend with Jesus before the resurrection and the reaching of our final destination in God involves being in the Father's resting place where we are refreshed and renewed in our fellowship life.

When Jesus was dying on the cross he turned to the penitent thief and said that on that very day they would both walk in paradise (Luke 23:43). Geldenhuys says that this passage is in complete agreement with the rest of the New Testament which clearly teaches that the saved immediately after death associates spiritually with Jesus in heavenly bliss.[10] Therefore the dead progress and mature in their faith because of this association with Jesus. This is certainly the burning desire of the apostle Paul when he says how he longs to depart and be with Christ.[11] The writer of the Hebrews seems to affirm this idea when he speaks of the 'spirits of righteous men made perfect' (Heb. 12:23).

This relationship with Jesus amongst the faithful dead also includes the sharing of hurt feelings and longings. John in his vision sees the martyrs of God calling out for the time of judgement to come (Rev. 6:9–11). Granted that this is poetic vision, it nonetheless affirms the New Testament teaching of continuing relationships with God for the dead. It also suggests to us that the dead are aware of events upon the earth. This is further affirmed by references to the prayers of the saints in heaven (Rev. 5:8ff; 8:3ff). On both occasions the prayers are of an intercessory nature because God is seen to answer their requests with a response of saving power or outpoured judgement. Of course the model for this continuation of prayer for others is that of Jesus himself whom we are told 'ever lives to intercede for them' (Heb. 7:25).

We now need to draw our conclusions from this evidence. Those who die in the faith of Christ certainly go on developing in their faith and relationship with Jesus. There is also some suggestion that they are to some degree aware of events amongst the living as their prayer life suggests. I do not think that we are stretching the evidence to say also that this process of continued growth will also be true of children and babies who have died. Indeed, a cursory gleaning of the gospels will give us an insight into the special care that Jesus had for children, whom he said would certainly populate heaven (Matt. 18:1–11). Personally, I find it extremely attractive to think of all the young whose lives were terminated so tragically receiving an education in the company of Jesus and the angels!

What we now need to ask is – if there is such a state of awareness amongst the dead – is there a legitimate way in which the living and the dead can either relate to or affect each other? Certainly there is a strong message running throughout the Bible that forbids such practices as spiritualism, witchcraft, and contacting the dead. The classic Old Testament passage for this is Deut. 18:10–12: 'Let no-one be found among you who . . . practises divination or sorcery . . . engages in witchcraft, or casts spells, or who is a medium or spiritist or who consults the dead.' The penalty for engagement in any of these practices was death.[12]

In the New Testament we are told that those who practise the occult (looking into things which God has hidden from us), will not inherit the kingdom of God (Gal. 5:20). Very often the parable of the rich man and Lazarus is used to underline this fact (Luke 16:19–31). In this story Abraham speaks to the man in torment in the underworld and says that it is not possible for the dead to return to life to warn the living, and that a gulf has in fact been fixed in the underworld between the righteous and the damned. Most commentators, however, say that this parable was not told to give details of the intermediate state of existence but rather to encourage the living to live by God's word. Therefore we can conclude that, for the Christian, the active seeking to establish a contact with the dead is forbidden to us. Yet this does not mean that when someone dear to us dies we work hard at forgetting them and not enjoy either our memory of them or their person. To a very large degree, such people have become a part of us, and the deposit of what they have given us goes on enriching our lives.

Finally in this chapter we must examine some of the records in the Scriptures which actually describe contact between the living and the dead. The vast majority of these are taken from the New Testament, and this should be no surprise to us when we consider that Jesus describes himself as the Resurrection and the Life. This will help us to come to some knowledge as to the nature of relationship which God himself has created between the living and the dead.

SAUL AND THE MEDIUM OF ENDOR   (1 Sam. 28:3–25; 1 Chron. 10:13–14)

The background to this account is that of the imminent defeat of the Israelite army at the hands of the Philistines. King Saul had been desperately trying to get a prophetic word from God but nothing seemed to be working out. The aged prophet Samuel was now dead and so there was a lack of the prophetic guidance to which Saul had been accustomed. Therefore, in desperation, Saul went in disguise to consult a medium at Endor. He asked that Samuel be brought up to him; presumably because he wanted a word of guidance even from beyond the grave.

It is what happened next that has caused much debate. According to the context it is apparent that the real Samuel had appeared (1 Sam. 18:12–15). Saul recognises the description given of the spirit and Samuel himself seems to be disturbed at the events as well. What also seems to indicate that it was the real Samuel is that the medium herself recognises the stature of Samuel, and this meant that the enquirer could be none other than Saul and so she feared for her life. If we take the story at its face value it now seems that a formal mediumistic procedure is abandoned as Samuel and Saul engage in direct conversation. Samuel utters a terrible prophecy of doom for the house of Saul and says that he and his sons will soon be joining him in the world of the dead. Judging from Saul's reaction to this encounter he is convinced he is meeting the real Samuel.

Dr H. L. Wilmington outlines some alternative suggestions as to whether this was the real Samuel or not:

1. The appearance of Samuel was a psychological impression
According to his view, the woman had permitted herself to become emotionally involved, and so psychologically identified with the prophet Samuel, and convinced herself that she had actually seen Samuel when she called him up. Alexander

Maclaren says a similar thing when he says that it matters not whether the woman brought up Samuel or whether she was as much awed as Saul was by the coming up of an old man covered with the well-known mantle, it is the prophecy of doom that we should take note of.[13]

There are two objections to this viewpoint. The medium cried out and was startled by the appearance of Samuel. Such would not be the case if she was psychologically identifying with the occasion. Second, as we have already noticed, Saul himself talked with Samuel.

2. This was a demonic impersonation of Samuel

Those holding this view suggest that whatever the outward form of the manifestation, it is but an impersonation of the real person. The defence for this approach is that God would not permit a woman of this type actually to disturb the rest of a godly man nor use her to convey the word of the Lord. After all, Satan can appear as an angel of light (2 Cor. 11:14). It is indeed true that many spiritistic phenomena are due to demonic spirits rather than to trickery or the psychic ability of the individual. However, it does not appear to be demonic in this case. First, God has used some rather unclean characters to convey his word to others on a number of occasions. Consider the testimony of the prostitute Rahab who witnessed the word of the Lord to the spies she hid in her house (Josh. 2:8–11). There is also the example of the high priest Caiaphas who prophesied the death of Jesus for the Jewish nation, and he himself was implacably opposed to Jesus' ministry (John 11:49–53).

It also seems doubtful that if this was demonic impersonation it would have contained such a rebuke to Saul and a reminder to do properly the will of God. If anything, it was Saul himself who was afflicted by demonic spirits as his attempts to kill David and Jonathan testify.[14]

3. This was a fake mediumistic encounter

This view is sustained only if we accept that the woman alone saw Samuel and that Saul heard and saw nothing. This hardly fits the evidence of Scripture. It is also highly improbable that the woman would have given such a word of doom to the king when her own life might well be forfeit as a result.

4. This was the real Samuel

Wilmington says that this is the most popular view and it is the only one which fits all the evidence of the account.[15] What, then, is the purpose of God in bringing the dead Samuel back to talk with the living Saul? It was certainly designed to emphasise the doom of Saul and the displeasure of God for his attempt to contact the dead through a medium. John J. Davis says that this is a completely unique event in the Bible and is not to be compared with the transfiguration encounter of Elijah and Moses with Jesus, because they appeared in glory whilst Samuel was clad in his old prophet's mantle.[16]

So we have here a contact between the dead and the living which God himself has commissioned for his own purposes. Whilst this does not give us a mandate to expect regular occurrences of the same, it does at least establish that God, for his own sovereign will, can arrange an encounter between the living and the dead. It also illustrates for us that sometimes the living feel they need a word from their dead and that the words of the deceased can exert a powerful influence upon the living. Yet we must be quick to say that all this needs to be within the boundaries of God's word and express will.

THE TRANSFIGURATION ENCOUNTERS   (Matt. 17:1–9; Mark 9:2–13; Luke 9:28–36)

Whatever the glory and splendour of this moment on the mountain with the transfigured Jesus, Peter is quite convinced that at least two of the Old Testament saints had come back to life.

He is sure that Elijah and Moses are not phantoms or elements of some vision he is having. He offers to build tents or booths for all three, so that the moment can be prolonged by a time of rest and shelter. Although Jesus does not contradict Peter's confession that 'it is good to be here' (Matt. 17:4), he nonetheless does not allow the encounter to become permanent in any way. Indeed, God's words, 'This is my beloved son in whom I am well pleased, listen to him,' suggest that whatever the importance of the occasion it must not overshadow our commitment to Jesus Christ as Lord.

There has been much speculation as to why these two people appeared to Jesus. The Lucan narrative says that they enquired concerning Jesus' departure, or death and resurrection, in Jerusalem. Some scholars see this event as a parallel to the deliverance gained by the exodus from Egypt to the land of promise. J. C. Ryle says that there can be little question that there was one main objective of this wonderful experience. It was meant to encourage the disciples by giving them a glimpse of good things yet to come.[17] Maclaren says that Moses and Elijah:

> . . . are witnesses of an immortal life and proofs that his (Jesus') yet unpierced hands held the keys of life and death. He opened the gate which moves backwards to no hand but his and summoned them; and they come, with no napkins about their heads and no trailing grave clothes entangling their feet, and own him as King of life . . . Now these two are brought from hopeful repose, perchance to learn how near their deliverance was; and behind them we seem to discern a dim crowd of holy men and women . . . who throng the portals of the unseen world, waiting for the near advent of the better Samson to bear away the gates to the city on the hill and lead thither their ransomed train.[18]

It seems quite logical that between them Moses and Elijah speak of the law and the prophetic word, both of which are come to completion in Jesus Christ. Others have attempted to see further significance in Moses and Elijah. For example, Ironside says that Moses represents those who, having died, will be raised in glorified bodies, and Elijah depicts all believers, who, at the Rapture, will be caught up into heaven without passing through death.[19] Be this as it may, the point we wish to make about the Transfiguration is that it is a meeting between the living, Jesus and his three disciples, and the deceased, no matter how mysterious their dying. There are those who believe this to be a visionary experience and refer to the mention of appearing glory. R. T. France says that the word *horama*, which is used by Jesus to describe the event, largely refers to an inward experience like a trance or vision.[20] However, the text does not support this use of the term here. The Lucan parallel mentions how the two men were on the point of leaving when Peter tried to delay their departure by offering to build shelters. This is hardly the response of a man undergoing a trance or a vision.

So what use can we make of this encounter between the dead and living. Again we accept that it is a sovereign moment called by God for his own purposes. It is also worth pointing out that Moses and Elijah appeared in order to talk with Jesus and not the disciples. Maclaren says that this event also teaches us that Jesus is the lord of all the living and the dead, and yet care must be taken in drawing dogmatic conclusions from a manifestly abnormal incident.[21] I do not think it is stretching the evidence to say that the only meeting between the dead saints and the living which are allowable are those sanctioned by God and which are centred upon the person of the Lord Jesus Christ.

THE HEALING OF LAZARUS   (John 11:1–44)

At first sight this might not strike us as a meeting between the living and the dead. Yet the fact of the matter is that Jesus spoke to a man who had been dead for at least four days. The dead man had had his funeral and been buried. Yet Jesus called out loud, for all to hear, including the dead, 'Lazarus, come out!' (John 11:43). The account continues, 'The dead man came out, his hands and feet wrapped with strips of linen, and a cloth around his face' (v. 44). Perhaps this account more than any other speaks to us of the power of Jesus Christ to reach out to the dead and give them words of life. Whilst we cannot use this passage to sanction any attempt to contact the dead, it does provide us with an encouragement that Jesus can speak to our dead and bring them his blessing.

John Hampsch says that in praying for our deceased relatives we must be careful not to evoke them, but only invoke God for them and their needs. 'We pray with them and for them but we are not allowed to talk to them or communicate directly.'[22] He goes on to say that very often, even after a person has died, we may find that we are still carrying grudges against them and may have to forgive them and, through Jesus, be forgiven on behalf of the deceased. He speaks of this as an unbinding of both the dead and the living, and uses the unbinding of Lazarus from his burial clothes as an illustration of this.

Another interesting use of the Lazarus story is found in the book *Healing the Greatest Hurt* by Matthew and Dennis Linn and Sheila Fabricant. They suggest that this episode offers us a model for healing a death. They offer the following outline.

1. *Share our heart with Jesus* (John 11:1–41)
Here Mary and Martha pour out their hurt feelings to Jesus. Doubtless they are sharing how much they miss their brother and mingle their anger and frustration with their sorrow. It is also encouraging to know that Jesus does not refuse such emotion but shares it with them; Jesus wept.

2. *Unbind and heal the deceased* (John 11:44)
Jesus spoke words of life to the dead, so, through Jesus, offer your own words of love and life to the deceased. This provides

an opportunity to speak out any words which have been unsaid for however long. We have already noted how the dead in Christ continue to develop and grow after death, therefore we can offer prayers through Christ for their continued healing.

3. *Give thanks for new life*   (John 11:42, 45)
Learn to include a spirit of celebration for the life of the dead. Such thanksgiving brings release to the living and joy to the dead.[23]

We can say that the living do really benefit from this kind of prayer because they are being enabled by the Lord Jesus to work through any unfinished material concerning their deceased. The benefits to the deceased cannot be measured by us and we do not have any real scriptural evidence by which we can estimate what happens as a result of our prayers. However, the Lazarus story tells us that Jesus can speak healing to the dead, and so we can trust him to speak such healing to our deceased as he wills in response to our prayers.

THE CLOUD OF WITNESSES   (Heb. 12:1, 22–4)

The cloud of witnesses mentioned here are obviously those departed saints mentioned in the previous chapter who had either conquered through faith or who were called upon to give their lives in sacrifice for their faith. All alike had now died and in the process of such were looking for a better city than earth had as yet allowed. Now the writer, in exhorting the Hebrew Christians to go forward in their faith, encourages the living by telling them that the deceased are watching their progress rather like spectators at the races in the amphitheatre. William Barclay says that the unseen cloud of witnesses are a witness in a double sense, 'for they have witnessed their confession to Christ and they are now witnesses of our perform-

ance. The Christian is like a runner in some crowded stadium.
As he presses on, the crowd looks down; and the crowd looking
down are those who have already won the crown.'[24] Some have
said that because the Greek word for witness is *martureo*, it
strictly means that the departed are not witnesses 'of us' but
witnesses 'to us'. However, with Maclaren we are bound to say
that such an idea of spectatorship is almost needed to give full
force to the exhortation and imagery. 'It does seem a bit lame
to say, you are like runners surrounded by a crowd of witnesses
and therefore run, only do not suppose that they really see
you. If this is so, the glowing imagery seems to receive a violent
chill, and the flow of exhortation to be much choked.'[25]

The obvious import of this passage is that we are not alone
in our race of faith and life. God is with us through his Holy
Spirit but we have the saints in heaven to witness our running.
We can only conclude that their watching is to pray and urge
us on. We have already glimpsed the fact that Revelation
speaks of the saints interceding for the needs on the earth.

> Surely there is love in heaven, and maybe there is knowledge
> and it may be there is care for us. At all events the thought
> may come with cheer to our hearts that, whether conscious
> of one another's mode of being or not, they in their triumph
> and we in our toils are bound together with real bonds.[26]

I can remember quite vividly watching television and learning
that a Christian friend of mine, Wendy White, an Elim missionary in Zimbabwe, had been brutally killed along with all her
fellow workers and their children. A week later I was sitting
in a charismatic prayer meeting in Upton Hall Convent in
Birkenhead when Sister Breda came in and said that in her
devotions God had just reminded her that we were all being
prayed for by Wendy who was now in heaven. I know it is only
a subjective feeling but I suddenly felt the rightness of what
she said and felt comforted by Wendy. I felt I just had to thank
God for his grace and his timely reminder that there is only

one body of Christ and that when you die you do not suddenly leave it.

This idea of the corporate fellowship of all saints, living and departed, is also reinforced by the passage which speaks of the living coming to '. . . thousands upon thousands of angels in joyful assembly . . . You have come to God . . . to the spirits of just men made perfect . . . to Jesus' (Heb. 12:22ff). Barclay treats this passage as dealing with the future benefits awaiting us in heaven. However, the setting is that of the present, and of Christians who in worship to the living God do not come alone before this throne. We come with the whole company of heaven. It is from texts like this that the modern Anglican and Roman Catholic liturgies of communion speak of worshipping with the gathered company of the saints. The ancient creeds speak of 'the communion of saints', and whilst obviously refer-ring to the living they do not in any way exclude the deceased. As I read this passage, I think we have, generally speaking, grievously blundered in severing heaven from earth. We think of these two spheres as being totally cut off from one another and having no communication with one another. And the human heart has taken its revenge for such a divorce of the heavenly and the earthly. I am not for one minute condoning or advocating spiritism, but I think we need to see that one of its reasons for being of popular interest is a need for fellowship with those who have gone before, the desire to prove that heaven and earth are in communication with one another. 'The only way in which we can combat spiritism is ourselves to rescue this truth about fellowship from the neglect into which it has fallen, to speak and think in a more Christian way about those who have passed on.'[27]

So these two passages remind us that we belong to a fellow-ship of saints of all ages. Whilst we may not be at liberty to speak to them we are called upon to acknowledge and recognise them as fellow heirs of God's promises. They, in their turn, offer us support and encouragement. At the head and centre of this ever increasing family is Jesus, the son of the Father.

THE SPIRITS IN PRISON   (1 Pet. 3:19, 4:6)

Before engaging on a discussion of this passage we need to clarify just where it was that Jesus was preaching. The Apostles' Creed refers to this passage with the words, 'He descended into hell'. The correct term is 'hades', and this term is the equivalent of the Old Testament word 'Sheol'. Hades was the place where all the dead went, hell is the place of punishment of the wicked. Hades, like Sheol, was a shadowy world where the spirits of people moved like grey ghosts in an everlasting twilight. As time went on there emerged the idea of stages and divisions in this shadowland. The story of the rich man and Lazarus reflects this Jewish idea of a gulf separating the righteous and unrighteous dead. The unrighteous dead were thought to be kept in a kind of prison house in which they were held until the final judgement of God.[28]

It is to this shadowy world of the dead that Jesus comes; he gives homilies in hades. There is some debate as to whether the spirits referred to are either angels or the departed spirits of people. Some scholars suggest that the term *pneumata* (spirits) is only used in this unqualified sense of supernatural beings and never of the departed.[29] Yet it is a fact that the term has been used of the human make-up in a variety of ways and seems naturally to refer to human beings at this juncture. This seems to be supported by the reference later on in Peter (1 Pet. 4:6) which specifically states that Jesus preached the gospel to those who were dead.[30]

Taking both of these passages together it seems that Jesus preached both specifically to those imprisoned for disobedience from the days of Noah and to the dead in general. Barclay suggests that perhaps one of the reasons for preaching to the righteous dead would be to lead them out of hades into the paradise of God.[31] In other words, Jesus was proclaiming his triumph fresh from Calvary, and this not only signalled the inevitable judgement of evil but the releasing of the captives who had been waiting for their full redemption. This is why, then, the Christian promise is made that, from now on, those that die in the faith do not go to the shadowland of hades but being absent from the body are present with the Lord in paradise. Perhaps this is also why, in Revelation 5:13 it is mentioned that those 'under the earth' also join in the song of redemption.

However, we need to ask what was the purpose of Jesus in preaching to the unrighteous dead? Is this in fact a second chance of salvation? Interestingly enough, Peter is very careful to include as part of this challenging passage the fact that Christ died once for all and that even the dead will have to face Jesus as their judge. This is in fact why the Gospel is preached in hades, in order to make very clear the offer of salvation and the fact of judgement to those who have rejected this Gospel. It almost seems to be the parable of Dives and Lazarus in reverse. Here there is no messenger to the living from among the dead, but a messenger from the living come down to the dead. B. F. Westcott in his book *Historic Faith* says that Christ in dying shared to the full our lot. His body was laid in the tomb. His soul passed into that state in which we conceive that our souls shall enter. He has won for God and hallowed every condition of human existence. We cannot be where he has not been. He bore our nature as living; he bore our nature as dead.[32]

We are not at liberty from this text to say that the unsaved are saved after they have died. I think we can say that the righteous are given a fuller glimpse of him in whom they have put their hope. I think too we can accept that the result of such a revelation is that they enter into that same glory of God from which Elijah and Moses appeared on that day of transfiguration. This preaching in hades is also to be seen as an act of love when the words of mercy and triumph are scattered in the pathway of those who have hoped, in the land of shadows, for a better day to dawn. Therefore this speaking with the dead is actually a completion of the work of the cross by which we who put our trust in Jesus as Saviour have been saved and delivered from our sins.

BAPTISMS FOR THE DEAD   (1 Cor. 15:29)

We come now to our final text which describes some form of meeting with the dead. The most natural understanding of this verse is that some of the early believers got themselves baptised on behalf of friends who had died without receiving the sacrament. R. St John Parry says that the plain and necessary sense of the words implies the existence of a practice of vicarious baptism at Corinth.[33] Parry goes on to say that for evangelicals the awkward thing is that, no matter how hard we try to dodge the issues of this passage, it is apparent that the apostle Paul refers to this practice without condemnation as a proof for the reality of the resurrection. However, it must be pointed out that Paul does not go on to commend the practice or mention it anywhere else in his writings. Barclay says that this custom sprang from a superstitious view of baptism, that without it, a person was necessarily excluded from heaven.[34] This is not strictly true as this kind of belief actually gave rise to infant baptism, whereas the early practice was to delay baptism to the last possible moment on the grounds that as the sacrament washed away all sins then there would be little opportunity for further sins to be committed.

I do not think that the intention of such baptisms for the dead was that they might be saved and delivered into heaven as the Mormon Church practises. Such views had not been developed by that time. The most likely explanation is that it was an act of love for the dead by the living. Many different reasons are suggested, such as the dead were martyred before they were baptised, or that the Christian faith was still in its primitive stage and that the importance of the rite of baptism had not been appreciated by the deceased. The practice died out in the later Church presumably because persecutions eventually ceased and the sacrament became more and more regularised in the life of the Church. Whatever the real reason, the passage needs to be understood as an act of commitment and love to the Christian dead. It is this point that I wish us to take for ourselves in this book. There is a tendency in the western Church, once the eulogies and the funeral service are over, to forget those who have died. We need to cherish our dead and make acts of remembrance and to thank God for them at proper times and seasons. Where appropriate, we need to love our saints and proclaim to them also the great truths of the Gospel in the name of Jesus who has led the way. As an evangelical serving in a parish which regularly reads out the names of the departed on the anniversary of their deaths, I must testify that I came to appreciate the real sense in which they were entering into the reality of the communion of the saints.

In this chapter we have been briefly reviewing the biblical insights into relationships between the living and the dead. We see that, whilst there is a definite ban on all forms of spiritualism, there is indeed a crossing of the boundary which separates these two parties in the person of Jesus Christ. He speaks to the dead in their world and allows them access to this according to his will and purpose. There is a place of meeting for the living and the dead in the body of Christ and in the context of worship of the living God. There is also mention of acts of love and commitment to the dead. There may be times when we may have to unbind our relationships with our dead, as the experience of Lazarus illustrates. We have seen that there is

also the occasional gap in this division when the dead stray
among the living, as the example of the dead Samuel illustrates.
We now have a basis for examining the way a Christian can
respond to people who say that they are troubled in some way
by those who have died. However, before we can do this we
shall now go on to look at how the Church developed these
ideas.

3

Prayers, Purgatory and Protestants

To understand the way Christian thought about the dead developed in the first century and beyond we will need first to look at what was going on in Jewish theology at the time of Jesus. In all this, I think it is helpful to try to put ourselves in the shoes of the early Christians who were seeking after truth, being open to the Spirit, learning from the teaching and ministry of Jesus, working from the foundations of their Jewish heritage, yet all the while looking at life and death in the light of the momentous event of the death and resurrection of the Messiah. As they moved out into the Greek world to evangelise, so they also faced the added complications of Greek thought about death. But note that they had not been through the rigours of the Reformation. There was no Catholic/Protestant divide in their theology of the dead, so they had the advantage of not being burdened by prejudice.

For the believer living in Old Testament times there was a hope of life after death (see Isa. 26:19), but it was a vague hope. What is clear however is that there was a sense of power about the dead. Numbers 19:11–22 gives some very clear instructions to the people of Israel about dealing with a dead body. It points out that it is absolutely vital to take every precaution in dealing with a body. Of course there is hygienic good sense in this, but we also need to remember that the ancient Hebrew was not separatist in his thinking about man as body, soul and spirit, and therefore he is aware that the dead body still has 'spiritual power'. It was reckoned that the

soul of the deceased remained near the body for three days
after death and indeed had some reference to the body until
total corruption had taken place. The body therefore was greatly respected, and the burial place was most important.

BETWEEN THE TESTAMENTS

The inter-testamental period was a very crucial time for the
development of thought about the dead. This was a time of
considerable turbulence for the Jews. The Apocryphal book of
Maccabees describes the exploits of some great heroes of faith,
and one outstanding hero is Judas Maccabaeus. In 2 Macc. 12
we read the story of Judas defeating Gorgias, the governor of
Idumea. Some Jews were killed in this battle and they needed
to be buried. The story continues from verse 38 as follows:

> After the battle Judas led his men to the town of Adullam. It
> was the day before the Sabbath, so they purified themselves
> according to Jewish custom and then observed the holy day.
> By the following day it was urgent that they gather up the
> bodies of the men who had been killed in battle and bury
> them in their family tombs. But on each of the dead, hidden
> under their clothes, they found small images of the gods
> worshipped in Jamnia, which the Law forbids Jews to wear.
> Everyone then knew why these men had been killed. So they
> praised the ways of the Lord, the just judge, who reveals
> what is hidden, and they begged him that this sin might be
> completely blotted out. Then, Judas, that great man, urged
> the people to keep away from sin, because they had seen for
> themselves what had happened to those men who had sinned.
> He also took up a collection from all his men, totalling about
> two kilograms of silver, and sent it to Jerusalem to provide
> for a sin-offering. Judas did this noble thing because he
> believed in the resurrection of the dead. If he had not

believed that the dead would be raised, it would have been foolish and useless to pray for them. In his firm and devout conviction that all God's faithful people would receive a wonderful reward, Judas made provision for a sin offering to set free from their sin those who had died.   (Good News Bible)

It is perhaps helpful to notice various things about this passage:

1. The custom was to bury the dead in a family tomb. It was seen to be necessary to keep the family together, even in death.

2. Their idolatry was seen to be the cause of the death of these men, and they needed to be cleansed from this.

3. Judas believed in the resurrection of the dead and has a stronger view about the afterlife than the Old Testament view.

4. Because he believed in the hope of afterlife, he saw it as necessary to pray for the men who had died in sin, believing that his prayer and the effect of the sacrifice would bring them freedom and their just reward.

Judas, living in the second century BC, was one of those to whom God was revealing the idea of the resurrection of the dead. It was all part of the Spirit, preparing people for the cross and resurrection of Jesus. We need to recognise that this sort of story, about one of the great heroes of the faith, was a very popular one among the Jews of Jesus' day, and it was normal to pray for the dead. The problem for some of the Jews, particularly the Sadducees, was that they could not agree which books, apart from the Torah, could be considered as holy Scripture. By the time of Jesus, those books known as the 'Prophets' had won acceptance, but those called the 'Writings' (which included the books of Maccabees) had not been unanimously accepted as canonical. However, Jesus freely quoted from them (including some of the apocryphal books) and during the first three centuries the Apocrypha was generally used in the Church. But in the fourth and fifth centuries several of the early Fathers did start to doubt their authority and preferred the Scriptures that had been written in Hebrew. Though Ambrose, Augustine and other prominent leaders defended these books, Jerome did not favour them and his influence was considerable. The apocryphal books were decidedly rejected by the Protestants at the Reformation, whereas the Roman Catholics upheld their acceptance at the Council of Trent in 1546. The Jews incidentally continue to pray for the dead, and in their prayer book there can be found such prayers as:

> May God remember the soul of my revered father (mother) who has gone up to his (her) repose. May his (her) soul be bound up in the bond of life. May his (her) rest be glorious with fullness of joy in thy presence, and bliss for evermore at thy right hand. (a prayer for the parent on the anniversary of their death[1])

JESUS AND THE DEAD

It is clear then, that at the start of the first century AD we have a Jewish community which, apart from the Sadducees, is very much alive to the hope of afterlife. The first-century priest and historian, Josephus, wrote a discourse to the Greeks outlining his convictions about the afterlife. As a Pharisee he had a clear belief in afterlife, and he believed that the soul, following death, goes to hades, a place where souls are detained after death. 'There is one descent into this region, at whose gate we believe there stands an archangel with an host . . . The just are guided to the right hand . . . the place we call the Bosom of Abraham.' The just therefore go to the bosom of Abraham, but as to the unjust, 'they are dragged by force to the left hand, by the angels allotted for punishment . . . These angels . . . drag them into the neighbourhood of hell itself.'[2]

Apart from the Sadducees, the Jewish people were at home

with the concept of the afterlife. The prayers for the dead formed a regular part of synagogue prayers, which raises the interesting question of what Jesus and the early disciples did when they were in the synagogue. Did Jesus pray for the dead? Did he join in the synagogue prayers for the dead, or did he shut his lips at that point? We can't base anything on this as it would be an argument from silence, but all we do know is that there is no recorded statement of Jesus opposing the custom. In his discussion with the Sadducees about resurrection (Matt. 22:23–33) he says to them, 'You know neither the Scriptures or the power of God.' God is powerful enough to make us as the angels after we die, and the Scriptures make it plain that the dead continue an existence after death. Jesus argues from Exodus 3:6 that the God who revealed himself to Moses, calls himself 'the God of Abraham, the God of Isaac and the God of Jacob', implying that Abraham, Isaac and Jacob are still very much 'alive'. The dead, far from being in some forgotten place, still have a reference to this life, not just as memories but as 'the living' ('God is not God of the dead but of the living').

The dramatic events of the first Easter and the Ascension gave a very clear foundation for Christian doctrine of salvation and the afterlife, but it was not a doctrine that was replacing the old, rather it was a natural development of it. Jesus had gone to heaven as the firstfruits, and believers who put their faith in Jesus as the Messiah could now have assurance of sins forgiven. They were made just by the blood of the Lamb and their destiny by grace was heaven.

For the early Church, the question of what to do with the dead was at first irrelevant, because they were expecting Jesus to return any day. However, as time went on it was clear that there might be a lapse of time before his return, and so it was natural for the Jewish practise of prayers for the dead to be accommodated into the Christian faith.

PRAYERS AND CULTS

As we consider how the early Christians developed their beliefs about the departed, we must always hold in mind that for them the separation between this world and the next was not seen to be as sharp as we might consider it. One of the places that marked the coming together of heaven and earth was the burial place of the deceased. Graves were not simply places where the body of the deceased lay 'a-mouldering', they were locations where in some mysterious way the soul was 'present'. It seems clear that in early church history it was common practice to gather at the tomb of the one who had died in the faith of Christ. This would be partly to do with respecting and remembering the death, and was a way of working through grief. It was also to do with a sense of drawing closer to the deceased so that they could ask them for their prayers, and they could ask God to bless them in Paradise.

Early tomb inscriptions give us some clue as to what happened at early funeral services. Take a look at the following:

'O Father of all, take into your keeping, Irene, Zoe and Marcellus whom you created. To you be the glory in Christ.' (catacomb of Priscilla dated between AD75 and 200)

'To our dearest Cyriacus, our sweetest son. May you live in the Holy Spirit.' (catacomb of Callixtus, AD200 to 300)

'Blessed Sozon gave back his soul aged 9 years. May the true Christ receive your spirit in peace, and pray for us.' (catacomb of Gordian and Epimachus, AD75 to 200)

'Pray for your parents Matronata Matrona, [you] who lived one year and 52 days.' (catacomb of the Lateran, AD200 to 300)[3]

I find these inscriptions very moving. They were not phrases chosen from the stonemason's handbook. A great deal of thought and feeling went into the composing of them, and they reveal the depth of love and feeling that the bereaved had for their loved ones who were dead but by no means forgotten. These inscriptions are really quite enlightening. They indicate that the following practices were normal in the early Church:

1. An act of commendation to God of the soul at death was normal.

2. A clear sense that the departed existed 'in the Holy Spirit'. Life in the Spirit is an experience of this world and the next.

3. Prayer was made for the departed, asking fairly general things such as requesting that the departed would enjoy peace and that they would be received by Christ.

4. It was assumed that one of the things that the departed would be doing in paradise, would be to pray for the living.

If you or I, then, had been a believer in those days and we had lost a member of our family or a dear friend, we would have taken them to an appropriate burial place, thanked God for them and prayed for them. We would respect the burial place and return there, especially at anniversaries of birthday and death, and continue to ask God to bless them, and to ask them to pray for us. There is no doctrine of salvation being achieved through the intercession of the living for the dead here. Salvation is clearly seen as being achieved by Jesus on the cross alone, and not by our prayers.

As time went on, special regard was given to the burial places of the martyrs, and there is no doubt that there developed a reverence and even mystique about these places. The burial places of the particularly pious became places of pilgrimage, churches were built over them (e.g. St Peter's in Rome), remains of their bodies became objects of devotion, and it became desirous to be buried as close as possible to the martyr, as this was reckoned to be of special benefit at the general resurrection. In many places this type of thing got badly out of hand, and the cult of the saints became a problem that church leaders had to face. There were terrible excesses, and one can't help feeling that the lovely simplicity of the early years soon got lost in superstition and sheer paganism.

What is interesting for our explorations, however, is the fact that the burial places of Christians of distinction were often places of spiritual power. It was not uncommon to hear testimonies of miracles, healings and deliverance taking place at the tombs of the saints. Thus Jerome, writing in the early part of the fifth century, records an astonishing episode that a pilgrim called Paula experienced when she visited the tombs of some prophets in the Holy Land:

> She shuddered at the sight of so many marvellous happenings. For there she was met by the noise of demons roaring in various torments, and, before the tombs of the saints, she saw men howling like wolves, barking like dogs, roaring like lions, hissing like snakes, bellowing like bulls; some twisted their heads to touch the earth by arching their bodies backwards; women hung upside down in midair, yet their skirts did not fall down over their heads.[4]

When I first came across this passage I read it with considerable interest, because I had been talking the day before with someone who had had a great deal of experience in deliverance ministry, and he had related to me a number of stories where the same phenomena occurred (I have to admit he did not include incidents of women hanging upside down!). Jerome would have believed these tombs to be so spiritually charged, that any demons coming near would have to flee. Hence, the deliverance phenomena.

The inscription on the tomb of Martin of Tours reads:

> Here lies Martin the bishop, of holy memory, whose soul is in the hand of God; but he is fully here, present and made plain in miracles of every kind.[5]

Such tombs were scenes of high activity, and there was a great expectation and faith for the miraculous. No doubt there was much which was very unhelpful and distracting about all this; I am much happier about the Church on earth being responsible for the healing ministry. But we must recognise that there was something powerful at these places. Was it demonic power, or the power of God? How on earth are we to understand these things?

Perhaps a way to view it is this: imagine a man who in this world shows himself to be a man filled with the Spirit. He exercises charismatic gifts including healing and deliverance, and he is noted for being particularly pious and living close to God. During his ministry here on earth, he has a powerful ministry of intercession. Through living close to his Father in heaven, he is able to see where God is at work, and he has the faith to move mountains. Once he has died, he moves to paradise, and here he is of course much closer to God. He is free of the effects of the fall, and he has entered the days of perfection. The argument would run: if in his days of imperfection he was able to be such a channel of blessing, then in his days of perfection, from paradise, his ministry of intercession would be even more effective and powerful. Because his burial place is like a sign on earth of his existence, the natural place to come to him would be the grave. The grave becomes a sacrament – the outward visible sign of the inward grace which, in this instance, is the man who has died in faith who now, unseen, is interceding for us. This assumes that you have some room for a belief that those in the world to come have some reference to those in this world. That is, we hold a belief that the saints pray for us.

I wonder if we in the twentieth century have something to learn from our Christian ancestors? I find myself very cautious about this, because the whole area is fraught with dangers. It seems to me that few in the early Church could handle all this without moving fairly quickly into some sort of worship of the saints and superstition. Spiritual power is something that man finds very difficult to handle. Even for Jesus, it was a temptation to use spiritual power for his own ends by throwing himself off the pinnacle of the Temple. It is a warning to us in these days when there is a wonderful release of God's power among us, that the Church down the centuries has often proved that it has been unable to handle it and has moved into idolatry.

In the case of our subject here, the power that for whatever reason, was evident at the tombs, soon became an object of fascination, and the dead – rather than being servants of the grace of God and being seen as intercessors – were soon being viewed as gods, and cults were developed. I feel sad as I view this piece of church history. One can't help feeling that these early Christians had discovered an important resource, but through misuse they in time lost it, and it provided material for heresy.

PURGATORY AND HERESY

As years went by a doctrine came into being which gave a whole new purpose to praying for the dead. This was the doctrine of purgatory. The *Oxford Dictionary of the Christian Church* gives the following definition for purgatory:

> According to RC teaching, the place or state of temporal punishment, where those who have died in the grace of God expiate their unforgiven venial sins and undergo such punishment as is still due to forgiven sins, before being admitted to the beatific Vision.

The Scriptures that have been used to support this doctrine are the passage from 2 Maccabees already referred to, and two New Testament passages which need to be looked at:

Matthew 12:31ff. This is the well known verse to do with the blasphemy against the Holy Spirit. This in itself has puzzled Bible commentators down the ages, but what is also puzzling is Jesus' comment that this particular sin cannot be forgiven, 'either in this age, or in the age to come'. I personally do not think you can build a doctrine on this because Jesus might simply be saying that sins will not be forgiven in the age to come whatever happens. However, many have interpreted this verse as implying a possibility for post-death forgiveness.

1 Corinthians 3:11–15. In this passage, Paul teaches that on the Day of the Lord our works will be revealed, by fire, to be made of either gold, silver, costly stones, wood, hay or straw. If it is one of the last three it will be burned up, and the burning will be painful. However, the person will still be saved, 'but only as one escaping through the flames'. This is all in the context of teaching about divisions in the Church and God wanting to build temples, founded on Christ and worthy habitations for the Spirit of God. Clearly in the Corinthian Church there was a fair bit of wood, hay and straw around, and Paul was needing to be clear about it. But exactly what is this burning-up process which takes place when 'the Day brings it to light'? Those who hold a view of purgatory would say that this passage argues a case for purgatorial fire, a refining process, whereby all unconfessed and undealt-with sin is cleared away in preparation for the face-to-face meeting with Christ. As we shall see in a moment, this view was summarily dismissed by the Reformers and by classical Protestantism.

But before we shout 'Amen', should we not pause and ask the question, 'Is there a truth here which got lost in heresy and anti-heresy hysteria?' We need to remember that purgatory has always been viewed as a process which believers have to go through on their way to heaven, and is not for those destined for hell. So it should not be seen as a means by which people earn their way into heaven. Purgatory is regarded as being necessary for the saved, not the unsaved.

We find a development of the idea of purgatory in the early

Church. Clement of Alexandria (died c.AD215) taught that those who repented on their deathbed but had no time to do penance in this life, would be sanctified by the purifying fire in the next.[6] Ambrose (died AD397) taught that those who have died await the end of time in different places according to their immediate fate which is decided by their works. Ambrose seems to be suggesting that there are waiting rooms of preparation before we enter heaven, and the waiting rooms represent different levels of purification. It was generally felt that martyrs had an immediate passage to heaven and did not have to go through purgatory. Augustine (died AD430) taught the absolute certainty of purifying pain in the next world in preparation for heaven.[7] Thomas Aquinas amplified the teaching on purgatory. He taught that the guilt of venial sin is expiated immediately after death by an act of perfect charity, but that the punishment had still to be borne. He believed that the tiniest pain in purgatory is greater than the most severe pain on earth, but people can bear it because of the assurance of salvation which gives the soul a deep peace. He taught that the prayers of the faithful on earth helped the souls of the faithful departed through the painful journey of purgatory. The official teaching of the Roman Catholic Church on purgatory was defined at the Councils of Lyons (1274) and Florence (1439).

Again, I need to make clear that this teaching of purgatory at every stage was a process seen to be appropriate for Christians, not unbelievers. Therefore prayer for those in purgatory was for hastening their passage through, not asking for their salvation. There was also a less clearly defined doctrine of 'limbo', which was understood as a type of in-between state. In Latin theology there was seen to be a condition known as 'the limbo of the fathers', which is of those who died at the time of the Old Covenant, and there was the 'limbo of the children', which is of such people as infants who die unbaptised. According to Augustine's view, they are in a state of original sin, but are innocent of personal guilt.

As we shall see in a moment, the doctrines of purgatory and limbo became greatly abused in the Middle Ages, and got well and truly thrown out by the Reformers. But again, it is perhaps interesting to note that, had we been members of the early Church, we would have held to a view of purgatory. Is there any truth in this that we need to pick up today?

It seems to me that there is room in the gospels for a belief in some sort of intermediate process between the moment of death and that moment when we shall see our Lord Jesus, face to face on that glorious day. Ken McAll calls this place not purgatory, but a convalescent home. His understanding is that we need a place where we can recover from the wounds of sin and come gradually into the light. Brother Ramon prefers to use the word, 'sanctificatory'. Ramon describes this process thus:

> I do not mean that there would be no suffering – but that it would not be penal, a suffering of retribution or payment, but rather the kind of suffering that the believer knows in this life as the Holy Spirit sears and burns him in the crucible of the divine Love.[8]

Ramon goes on to do a type of exposition of Newman's 'Dream of Gerontius', which describes the journey through death. When Gerontius dies, he is met by the angel who has guided him all through his life, and this angel leads him through the process that enables the interior transformation to take place where he can see face to face the 'Holiest in the height'. Ramon is someone who is held in respect by a very wide cross-section of Protestants, and I think it is the case that the breaking down of the iron curtain between protestant and catholic has meant that we have been able to look a little more closely at this doctrine of purgatory in an open way, rather than concentrating on guarding the walls.

What can we believe about purgatory? It is my view that we need to drop the word purgatory as it has too many unhelpful connotations. I like Ken McAll's idea of the convalescent home, and one might be right in saying that this place is actually paradise. I have been greatly helped in my understanding of life after death by Jim Graham's *Dying to Live*.[9] His understanding of Scripture leads him to conclude that there is a type of two-stage process that takes place after death:

1. At death, we leave our bodies and become discarnate spirits. Those who are saved, like the thief on the cross, go immediately to paradise. Paradise is a Persian word and means an exquisite garden. This new garden of Eden is the place of waiting, a place of great beauty, a type of foretaste of things to come. For the unsaved, their destination is hades, the prison referred to in 1 Peter 3:19. Again, it is a place for discarnate spirits. Gardens in the Bible are always places full of significance and imagery. There is the first garden, the garden of Eden, a place of such promise, and yet the place of temptation and the scene of the fall of mankind. There is the garden of Gethsemane, the place of agony, the place of Jesus accepting the will of the Father and setting his face to the cross. It is the place of prayer and the dark night of the soul. Then there is the Easter garden, the place of resurrection and transformation. It is the spring garden of hope, where the rivers of life flood over the drab wilderness of death. Paradise is the ultimate garden. In paradise there is the beauty of Eden and the resurrection glory of the Easter garden. And maybe there is also a Gethsemane part to this garden, that refining process whereby all that is against the will of God in us is taken away, and we are made perfect by the blood of the lamb. Paradise is the place where our bodies sleep, but our spirits remain active and very much alive.[10]

2. The second stage is where our bodies awake. This will be the general resurrection. Just as Jesus spent some time in paradise as a discarnate spirit, and then went on to become

reunited with his transformed earthly body, so we also will enjoy a resurrection body (1 Cor. 15). To use Jim Graham's picture, this is moving from the garden into the house, the house of many mansions. This is heaven, the proper place for those who are redeemed. Here we exist for eternity enjoying the full presence of the Lord. This is the place of the new heaven and the new earth. For the unsaved, they move from the prison of hades to hell. As I understand it, hell is the place of full separation from God, and that means there can be no life, and therefore means annihilation. This is the ultimate sadness for creatures which have been destined for eternity, but God has designed it that he will be perfectly just, and choices that individuals have made here on earth will be honoured in heaven.[11]

In all this then, I am arguing that at death, those who are saved will enter paradise in a discarnate state. Paradise will include some sort of refining process which is described in 1 Cor. 3:11–15. This has nothing to do with our destiny, but it is to do with preparation and holiness. It is the convalescent home, the 'sanctificatory' where that which was begun when we first came to Christ will be completed. All this is in preparation for that most wonderful of days when, fully perfected and more alive than we have ever been in this world, we shall dwell with God in the new heaven and the new earth.

PROTESTANTS AND PREJUDICE

It is very hard for those who are Protestants to think dispassionately about the subject of purgatory and prayer for the dead, because this was one of the key subjects that brought about the Reformation. By the fourteenth century, this doctrine had been dreadfully corrupted; the evil practices of selling indulgences had developed, and the poor and vulnerable were manipulated by threats about purgatory. Few of the faithful looked forward to heaven, as the prospect of a horrendous journey through purgatory filled their minds. Salvation and purgatory had got confused, and the simple gospel truth of salvation by faith had long been lost. Indulgences and prayers for the dead were seen as means of winning God's favour and achieving salvation, and it is probably true that for many the message of the cross was lost.

It is not surprising then, that when the bright new light of the reformers swept across Europe, fuelled by the rediscovery of salvation by faith alone in the atoning work of the cross, that this particular doctrine should have been one of the first to be attacked. Quite rightly, the terrible abuses were dealt with, and great freedom was brought to the faithful. Perhaps we cannot fully appreciate what a liberation this was. Few of the reformers were in the frame of mind to explore these doctrines any more closely than they had to. There was to be no turning back, no giving of ground to anything other than the gospel of salvation by faith.

Prayers for the dead then dispersed from the life of the Protestant Church. Cranmer did include a prayer for the deceased in his 1549 rite, 'At the Burial', which asked that the 'sinnes whiche he committed in this world be not imputed unto him, but that he, escaping the gates of hell and the paynes of eternall darkness may euer dwell in the region of lighte'. This prayer was taken out by 1552. Generally prayers that focused on the dead were seen to undermine the work of the cross. People were saved in this life, and there was no possibility of salvation after this life. Because they viewed prayer for the dead as being prayer for the salvation of the departed soul, they clearly had no time for it. The doctrine started to gain currency again when the Tractarians reintroduced the idea of purgatory, and called it 'the intermediate state', and it is on this that Newman based his 'Dream of Gerontius'.

There was also one other occasion that saw a revival in

prayer for the dead, and that was the severe and agonising experience of bereavement faced by millions of families during the First World War. R. J. Campbell wrote in 1916 that he believed the war would bring back a more definite doctrine of the communion of saints. Protestantism had 'little comfort to give to mourners, for it has been so sadly silent regarding the fate of our dead'.[12] During the war some of the strongest evangelicals changed their views about prayers for the dead. Alan Wilkinson writes:

> Bishop Moule of Durham, a staunch Evangelical, though he deplored medieval practices, said that he gave 'perpetual greetings' to the departed; it was certainly 'no sin' to follow them with '*suspira*' that they might enjoy ever-growing light and joy in heaven.[13]

In 1917 Archbishop Randall Davidson actually wrote and issued a prayer for the deceased, which was an explicit prayer for deceased soldiers that they might be 'accounted worthy of a place among the faithful servants in the Kingdom of heaven'.[14] Of course this was coming straight out of the 'valiant hearts' theology that those who gave their lives for their country were in a mysterious way identified with Christ who gave his life for the world. There were many critics of this quasi-Islamic belief but, nonetheless, the practice of praying for the departed was widespread and gave great comfort to many. It does support the view that those who are in grief do have a legitimate need to find ways of appropriately continuing a relationship with a deceased loved one and to find Christian ways of expressing it.

When we talk about relationships with our Roman Catholic brothers and sisters, we find that sooner or later we come up against these doctrines, and it is often at this point that we discover that our beliefs are not based on truth but on prejudice. Talk to many of an evangelical persuasion and they will dismiss any notion of praying for the dead, and will usually not take kindly to discussion on purgatory. But I want to ask, how much serious thinking have they done about the subject? Have they listened to the Catholic point of view? Is their belief based on a genuine searching for the truth, or on prejudices which have been uncritically absorbed into their subconscious?

As we enter this decade of evangelism, those of us who associate with charismatic renewal will be finding ourselves doing our evangelism with Catholics. What will happen, when we are witnessing door-to-door with a Catholic, and the subject of heaven comes up? Or what if someone asks whether they can pray for a deceased relative? We shall need to be prepared, and we will need to seek truth together.

It is my belief that there is ground between Catholic and Protestant views about the dead which we can move to. But it will mean dealing with some of our prejudices, and there are roots of bitterness which started four hundred years ago which still require healing.

So where has all this got us? We have travelled speedily through history, and are we any the wiser? I am conscious that I have raised more questions than I have answered, and on these sort of issues I find the fence a peculiarly attractive place upon which to sit. However, having explored the territory, I think we have made a few discoveries:

1. It soon becomes clear that, in approaching a subject like this, it is essential to exercise humility. We are all going to have lots of surprises when we die and find out what the other side is really like. It would be foolish to try and claim too much. We need to be humble in our attitude to others. The doctrines discussed above are held very dear to many of our Christian neighbours, and they are worthy of respect. We will need to listen and to learn and there will be time when we may have to let go of things that we have cherished uncritically over many years. We must invite the Spirit of all truth to lead us.

2. It seems to me that it does not run counter to biblical truth to admit to some sort of purifying process in paradise. I don't think we can claim much more than that. But if this is the case, it should encourage us all the more to see that the process of healing, wholeness and holiness is going on in this world. I actually take a lot of comfort from the thought that after death there will be a time of preparation before I meet Jesus. To use rather a trite analogy, I would rather go to my wedding having had a good shower, and changed into the proper clothes, rather than turning up dirty and in my working clothes, even though I know I am loved and accepted whatever I am wearing. Maybe the changing process will take a split second, maybe it will take longer – who knows, and what does time mean anyway in paradise!

3. Early tradition supports the practice of prayers for the dead. These prayers were not prayers to affect the salvation of the deceased. Rather they were acknowledging that they were still part of the community of faith, but no longer on earth but in paradise. There seems to me to be nothing wrong with offering prayers to God for the deceased which essentially expresses our love for them and our hope that they are enjoying peace in Christ. Pastorally, this may be a most helpful practice for those who are suffering bereavement. This needs to be treated with some caution as I foresee two dangers.

First, there are some people who need to be helped into a proper letting go of the deceased, and so this kind of prayer may be unhelpful for them. (However, some people find it hard to let go precisely because there is no obvious way of remembering the deceased. To pray in the way I have described may actually help the letting-go process. So discernment will be needed.) Secondly, for those who are not committed Christians, encouragement to pray for the dead may raise hopes that salvation can be procured after death. Folk religion thrives on such things, and we need to see that this is a discipline for the faithful.

4. Prayers by the dead is something that most Christians probably believe in. Most understand the 'cloud of witnesses' in Hebrews 12:1 as being the company of faithful who are, so to speak, in the grandstand cheering us on. It seems to me that there is a tremendous resource here. For all its faults, the early Church was probably on to something when they recognised the spiritual power in the prayers of the saints. The difficulty comes in knowing how to avail ourselves of this prayer backing. Do we need to ask, or is it there automatically? Do we ask the saints direct, or do we ask Jesus? I think we need to recognise the very real problems associated with direct requests to saints. Very quickly, it seems, such a practice moves us away from concentration on Jesus, and at its worst we can make gods of the saints. My feeling is that we do need to recognise the strength of this backing, and just as we might ask God to send his angels to defend and help us, so there can be an appropriate place for asking him to urge the saints to pray for us. This is not just a theological nicety. We are living in days when the spiritual battle is intense, and I believe it is in this realm of the spiritual battle that the prayer backing of the saints can be so helpful. Imagine people like the Wesleys, C. T. Studd, Arthur Wallis, David Watson and others, all people of great faith when they were here on earth, who now no longer see through a glass darkly, but who see perfectly and can pray perfectly for us. They can see the principalities and powers in ways that we can't. We know what prayer warriors they were when they were on earth, just think what they are like now! I am not being flippant here – I am pointing out that there is a tremendous resource of strength here for when we are engaged in the battle. This should encourage us.

5. The company of heaven knows how to worship the Lord. There are many references in the book of Revelation to the

faithful worshipping the Lord. I love the part of the Anglican Communion Service where we remind ourselves that we are in the company of 'angels and archangels and all the company of heaven', and together, in some way mystically joined in our act of worship, we utter together, 'Holy, Holy, Holy Lord, God of power and might . . .'. It lifts my spirit when I come into worship to think I am joining that great worship that is going on in paradise.

6. Any talk of paradise or heaven must inevitably excite the hope within us. In the West our vision of the afterlife is often very feeble. The early Church was fired by a clear, wonderful, unassailable vision of heaven. We need to dwell on the things of heaven, not as escapism, but rather to deepen our involvement in this world. We are the citizens of heaven who bring the good news of another kingdom to a world which has lost the vision. The disciple is one who is called to be a visionary, to carry in his or her heart the highway to Zion. Those who have such a highway in their hearts are the ones who are able to walk through even the valley of tears and turn them into springs of life. Those who have some understanding of the things of heaven 'go from strength to strength, till each appears before God in Zion' (Ps. 84:7).

4

Hurtings and Hauntings

AN UNEXPECTED VISITOR

It was a warm summer night and I awoke in the small hours. I was living at this time in an old house in Buckinghamshire, part of which dated back to the thirteenth century. I was alone in the room, but I awoke because I sensed I had company. Instinctively I felt afraid, because there was that curious sense that something supernatural was happening. I looked across to the far window, and there, as calmly as the summer night itself, stood a man, reading by the light of the moon. He wore a cloak and his stooped head supported a wide-brimmed hat. I felt terrified! Within moments the man had gone and I was alone in my room again, praying fervently and longing for the dawn!

Now the question is, what exactly did I see? At that time I was about twenty years old, I was a keen member of my university Christian Union, and in those days things were either black or white. What I had seen had frightened me, and the evangelical/pentecostal teaching that I had received on this sort of thing was that ghosts were evil and were a demonic impersonation. So, academically if you like, I was satisfied that I had been subject to a spiritual attack. This is one perfectly plausible explanation, and one I stood by for some time. But I was not entirely satisfied, and I found myself daring to probe a little deeper into this phenomenon, all the while anxious that I should not slide down the slippery slope into spiritualism.

There developed a type of ongoing debate in me which ran like this:

'The man was a messenger of Satan, a demon disguised and the purpose of this was to terrify you.'

'Well, that may be true, but on the other hand, I cannot deny that this man had no evil intention that I could make out. In fact he seemed quite gentle and did not really seem to notice me.'

'That's just how spiritualists talk. They make out that all this stuff about the dead is really very safe and attractive. Go further down this track and you will soon find yourself approaching mediums and trying seances to contact the man.'

'I loathe the thought of going off to seances in an attempt to contact this man or any dead person for that matter; I am simply trying to suggest that this "thing" may not have been a demon, but may have been a departed human spirit which for some reason, best known to himself, turned up in my bedroom on that particular night.'

And so the argument would go on.

The interesting little detail that did emerge some time after this incident is that I discovered that the house where we lived had been a popular meeting place for Quakers, and even George Fox himself stayed there. When I looked up drawings of Quakers they were dressed very similarly to my gentleman. And so, I ask, was this the spirit of one of the early Quakers?

Now I relate this incident because it is my impression that very many people have their own personal stories to tell about ghosts, and a lot of Christians are in fact afraid to talk about these experiences for fear that they will receive condemnatory statements in return. For many Christians, there is actually quite a loneliness in experiencing a supernatural or psychic experience of this sort. They may be suspected of having spiritist tendencies, or being demon-possessed, or simply rather odd, and not quite the sort of person one should be having fellowship with.

Because the experience is common, we need to work hard at understanding the phenomena, and we have to learn how to pastor those who need to relate such experiences in a safe environment.

WHAT IS A GHOST?

So what exactly is a ghost? How can we make sense of such phenomena? Using the above story as an example, there are five popular explanations:

1. Psychological
There would be those who would say that my experience was a type of vivid hallucination. They might say that this was like an extension of a deeply felt dream, and with the help of shadows playing tricks, a rich dinner and a lively late-adolescent mind, I believed I saw something that in reality was not there. There is no doubt that in some circumstances, such as severe grief, the internal power of longing can be so strong that it becomes hard to distinguish fact from fantasy.

Parapsychologists refer to a phenomenon known as 'crisis apparition', which describes that experience when one person in one particular place 'sees' someone they know who is in another place, and who is in some kind of trauma, or may be dying or have recently died without the other person being aware of it. I can remember a close friend describing this kind of experience: her husband was travelling away from home on business. In the night she was awoken by a terrible dream in which she saw her husband reaching out to her, appealing to her for help. Moments later she got the phone call to tell her that her husband had died from a heart attack in the night whilst staying in a motel. She never knew how to understand this experience and felt distinctly uncomfortable about telling this story in Christian company.

In 1987 the Christian Exorcism Study Group produced a report called *Deliverance*, subtitled 'Psychic Disturbances and Occult Involvement'. It states:

> The generally accepted explanation among para-psychologists is that such crisis apparitions do not involve the perception of a quasi-material 'ghost' or 'astral body' of the second person, but result from the first person receiving some sort of (telepathic?) message which is then exteriorized in apparitional form, sometimes at the very moment of crisis, but sometimes delayed by a number of hours or even days.[1]

What we are presented with here, then, is the possibility that the mind has considerable power to imagine the presence of another in such a way as to actually experience with one or more of the senses the presence of another who may be dead or in a different place. There is also the possibility of a communication between minds that is commonly called telepathy.

It is worth noting here, that there will be in most churches Christian folk who have some psychic or paranormal experience about which they feel uneasy and yet find it hard to share. The difficulty in sharing comes from the feeling that others within the Christian community will make judgements about them, which can be very hurtful. If they have shared these experiences at school they may well have been laughed at, ostracised or considered to be involved in witchcraft. This can make people very wary of sharing their experiences. I can recall several occasions when people have come to me, owning up to such experiences and sharing it as a deep burden. The burden is increased by all the teaching (albeit necessary) about the horrors of the occult. I remember one person who for many years had premonitions of disasters, and this was a psychic gift she could well have done without. It came to a head for her when she had a premonition of the sinking of the 'Herald of Free Enterprise' and she came to me for help. Together in prayer we offered this unwanted ability to God and I prayed for her to be cleansed from this psychic power. The result was that she became free of it and also felt a new freedom in her Christian life. She was one who found freedom, but my guess is that there are many more who are fearful of sharing such things in the Christian fellowship. We need to allow people to share their stories without threat of condemnation, so that they can experience the freedom of Jesus.

Under this heading then, we are acknowledging that many curious things go on in the mind which is subject to hallucination and psychic disturbances of one sort or another. It is possible therefore that ghost phenomena, such as my Quaker gentleman, was a product of the complexities of my mind and may indicate a weakness or area of unwholeness that needs cleansing and healing.

2. Place memory

This explanation of ghosts works on the assumption that some places are charged with memories from the past which can be picked up and projected out on to the present. There is no clear way of understanding or explaining this, but it does seem to be the case that certain places do attract ghost activity where the particular ghost, when sighted or heard, is doing the same thing over and over again. It can be compared with the experience when listening to a radio of suddenly picking up, quite unexpectedly, a message from a police patrol car. You think you are tuned into Radio 2, but suddenly find that you are listening for a few seconds to something totally different. In the same way, we are 'tuned' to pick up the wavelength of the here and now, but just occasionally some people have an ability to pick up something from the past. Some people just happen to be receivers of this type of 'memory', and they project it in such a way that they, and sometimes other observers, may witness a scene from the past. They observe something like a clip of a video film – that is, not the real thing, but an impression of it. To go back to my Quaker, the understanding according to this definition would be that I was experiencing a memory, a sort of photograph of this gentleman, and something about me at that particular time triggered this 'memory' into being. I have found no adequate way of testing this theory scientifically, but I can see some sense in it.

3. Impersonation

I mentioned that in my late teens and early twenties I had what I thought was a clear-cut understanding of ghosts, and the book which influenced me more than any other was *The Challenging Counterfeit* by Raphael Gasson. This was a book written by a man who once was deeply involved in spiritualism as a medium and had a considerable knowledge and experience of spiritualist and psychic phenomena. Following his dramatic conversion to Christ, he renounced his old ways and his book is an attempt to present the Christian gospel of truth and hope over against the deceptions of spiritualism. The book has undoubtedly helped many and has been a very significant publication in the Christian anti-occult literature.

The conclusion he comes to in his understanding of ghosts is that they are demons impersonating the spirits of dead relatives, and their main purpose is to seduce people into the bondage of spiritualism. He argues very convincingly that Satan has a well developed system of counterfeiting the spiritual gifts and is out to deceive all who stray near to this dangerous path. The spirits who communicate through mediums are, according to Gasson's understanding, clearly demonic:

> In view of the statements of Scripture which must remain the only measuring rod for all true Christians, there is only one conclusion that a Christian can arrive at, and that is that the spirits which so communicate, are not highly evolved 'spirit guides' and the souls of dead persons, but actually demons impersonating dead people. This may sound strange and unreal to those who have little or no contact with the

principalities and powers of darkness, but to the student of Scripture, it is no new thing . . . The demons, pretending to be the spirits of the departed, have to tread very carefully and they begin in a very plausible way and gradually ensnare those who are investigating out of mere curiosity.[2]

There is no doubt in my mind that spiritualism is an occult religion and completely contradicts all the glorious biblical truths about the promise of the afterlife. Nothing in either the Old or New Testament suggests that believers may go round trying to make contact with the dead.

Given, then, that spiritualism is occult, does it necessarily follow that all ghost phenomena are demonic impersonation? There is clearly teaching in Scripture about deceptive spirits and the need to discern the spirits, and this certainly suggests that in the spiritual realm nothing can be taken at face value. The powers of deceptiveness are strong. Demons in the New Testament generally manifest themselves as unseen destructive forces operating in individuals' lives, rather than disguising themselves as ghosts. But nonetheless, given the existence of demons, and given the deceptive nature of spiritualism, there is a very strong likelihood that mediums do make contact with demonic influences which can impersonate the relatives of the dead.

The conclusion I have personally come to is this: some mediums have occult powers to enable them to make contact with deceiving demons who disguise themselves as the dead relatives of those present or as the spirit of some significant person who has died and has something 'important' to communicate to the living. The ouija board has become a popular medium through which people try to make contact with the dead. In my teenage years I remember being invited to be part of a group who were using a ouija board (to be precise I think it was an upturned glass on a table which in some ways made it even more mysterious – did the spirit climb inside the glass, one wondered?). We were all rather alarmed when the spirit informed us that his name was 'Winston'. As Winston Churchill had died only a short while before this incident, we were quite convinced it was he, but we could think of no questions important or intelligent enough to ask of such a distinguished visitor, and my excursion into ouija was brought to an abrupt end! I do want to hastily add that I have since renounced the playing around with ouija and recognise the sinister powers that can be at work in this. I also feel I need to say, that in this particular case the glass was probably moved by us rather than an unseen force, but it is the sort of situation where some malignant spirit could ensnare some unsuspecting schoolboys, who thought they were communicating with a departed spirit. In fact not long after this another group of pupils tried with the glass and one of the boys was very badly affected and had some sort of a fit as a result. He had clearly made contact with a demonic power.

It may also be that some mediums do actually make contact with departed spirits. If this is the case they will make contact with the unquiet dead (see next section), rather than those who are resting in peace. Where this happens, the medium becomes guilty not so much of deception, but of cruelty, because the proper contact with any such dead should be to send them away from this world, not to continue to hold them here.

Dr Kenneth McAll, in his *Healing the Haunted*, tells the story of a family who moved into a large house in the south of England. The house had been the home of a well known spiritualist writer, who had since died. The house had a reputation for being haunted by this man, who apparently came back looking for his diary. When the family experienced various manifestations which suggested that the dead writer was still around the house, the father visited the vicar who came in and said prayers of release around the house. The house became peaceful, and there were no further manifestations of this kind. Interestingly, not long after this, a short article appeared in a daily newspaper reporting that a medium had received a message from this writer, apologising for having misled people during his life. McAll also adds:

> A few days later, a short article appeared in the *Daily Mail* saying that Madame Roberts, a famous medium in Kent, had at last received a message from this writer. Before he died he had promised that he would come back but never had done so and no one had ever 'met him' or heard anything from him, in spite of many attempts to arrange meetings. Now he was saying to the medium, 'I wish to apologise for having misled people during my life.[3]

In this instance it seems that Madame Roberts was successful in contacting the deceased, and perhaps in this instance it was permitted by God so that she might be brought to truth.

The conclusion thus far, therefore, is that in the world of spiritualism, mediums do often make contact with deceptive spirits or demons which impersonate the dead. But this is not universally the case, as there appear to be some geniune examples of the dead being contacted. The dead who are contacted are reckoned to be among the 'unquiet dead'.

I have written so far about contacts through mediums. There are of course many contacts with the dead which have nothing to do with mediums and spiritualism. Here I return to my test case of the Quaker. Was this ghost a demon impersonating a Quaker, as I believed at the time? Presumably, if it had been demonic impersonation, the intention was to either frighten me or to lure me into the fascination about the dead and therefore into spiritism or some other stream of the occult. The experience certainly frightened me, though I do wonder a bit why the demon had to disguise himself as a Quaker in order to frighten me. Could he not simply appear as himself, or play other nasty tricks? And although I was frightened, I was frightened not so much of the thing, as of the fact that I was witnessing something supernatural. The testimony of some of those who saw angels in the Bible is that they were terrified (see

Matthew 28:4 where the guards on the tomb of Jesus who saw the angels were so terrified that they became like dead men). So the fact that I was frightened, does not necessarily mean that the thing was evil. On the possibility that this experience was intended to lure me into spiritualism, I can only say that I wasn't! There is of course no foolproof test one can do to say whether or not this was demonic. The main guide comes from a gift, mentioned in 1 Corinthians 12:10, which distinguishes between different kinds of spirits, and unfortunately for us Western cerebral thinkers, this gift comes from that subconscious area of instinct and intuition which of course makes it 'unreliable'. Or does it? The Bible never puts a higher value on the more cerebral gifts. But there is no denying that when we come into the area of intuition it is harder to talk about things like 'proof' and 'certainty'. However, I would venture to say, that according to my intuition which I think may house some God-given ability to distinguish spirits, my impression is that this night-time visitor who came to my home was not a demon.

4. The 'unquiet dead'

The report, *Deliverance*, contains a chapter on the unquiet dead, and argues that ghost phenomena may well be appearances of the spirits of the dead, the souls of those departed this life who are not at rest and are therefore said to be 'unquiet'. The counsellor who is helping someone who is troubled by such a phenomenon

> . . . is forced to consider as a possible hypothesis that some particular and identifiable individual, though departed this world, is 'earthbound', and keeps troubling a person or place with which during his life he had particularly strong emotional ties. The ghost of someone may be seen in the place where he lived or worked or died, and his appearance may be observed by independent witnesses who sometimes

do not know him or the circumstances of his life and death until they make inquiries and discover them. In many cases the person whose ghost is seen will have died suddenly, tragically, or unexpectedly.[4]

The report goes on to say that the spirit of a dead person may manifest itself in this world for one of three possible reasons:

(a) the spirit has been too strongly attached to a place or person before death and cannot let go; it resents the present occupier of its beloved place and resents the making of new relationships from which it is now excluded;

(b) the spirit is distressed at being trapped in this world and is attracting attention as a cry for help;

(c) the spirit may be giving comfort as best it can to a person whom it has loved dearly and who is missing its physical presence.

According to this definition, then, the apparition that I saw was actually the soul of a departed Quaker. For some reason this man, following his death, had got trapped in some sort of limbo world where it was possible for him, on occasions, to appear to the living. Maybe this particular window was one that he strongly loved. Maybe he died a tragic death. Maybe he was trying to call my attention to release him to the afterlife. It is this category that particularly interests Dr McAll, and our next chapter deals more thoroughly with this.

This way of associating the dead with a type of 'limbo' land is not easy for evangelicals to digest. It does not fit neatly into our established ways of thinking about death and the afterlife. But my feeling is that our efforts to make the thing neat and tidy have restricted our vision, and certainly when one is dealing with the afterlife it would be foolhardy to try to be too neat and tidy. Obviously there is a great deal which is mysterious and unknown here, and we have to speculate. The fact is that these psychic phenomena do exist, they do trouble people and sometimes disturb them very deeply, and we do need to find ways of understanding them so that we can deal with them.

There is another side to this too. If, using the example of my Quaker, he really was a discarnate spirit, an unquiet dead, appealing to me for help, then this brings in a whole new area of responsibility for me. It means that I have responsibility towards not only the living but to the dead.

As someone who is in holy orders this is nothing very new for me. At every funeral service I take, I am responsible for commending the soul to God. In the case of the Quaker, had I entered into some sort of requiem, I would be simply doing what I would normally do at a funeral service, only many years after the death.

5. *Legitimate appearances of the dead*

We have looked at how ghost phenomena may be discarnate spirits 'stuck' in this world against their will who need some sort of help from us to release them. There is one last category, which is the discarnate spirit sent back to this world legitimately. That is, it seems that there may be occasions where God chooses to communicate something crucial to someone on earth, and he chooses one of the company of heaven to achieve this. In chapter 2 we looked at some biblical examples of this, notably the visit of Moses and Elijah to Jesus at the Transfiguration.

I have often been intrigued by the strange events going on in Jerusalem following the death of Jesus as recorded by Matthew. So momentous was the act of Jesus giving up his spirit that it had a dramatic effect on nearby matter (earth shook and rocks split), and Matthew reports that 'the tombs broke open and the bodies of many holy people who had died were raised to life. They came out of the tombs, and after Jesus' resurrection they went into the holy city and appeared to many people' (27:51–3). What are we to make of that? I have yet to find a satisfactory explanation for these tantalising verses. I would not want to draw too many conclusions, but I do note various things:

(a) The incident happened in connection with the separation of Jesus' spirit from his earthly body, and with the union of his spirit with his resurrected body.

(b) Matthew particularly points out that the bodies of the people rose. We are dealing therefore with resurrected bodies not ghosts.

(c) He also mentions that we are dealing with holy people going into a holy city. The absence of sin is interesting. The point of this exercise seems to be that some selected holy people were called by God to declare the glorious truth of the victory of Jesus over death.

This does seem to suggest that there are cases of a legitimate visit by the departed to someone in this world. There are of course a number of testimonies to this effect. When I was a curate I remember having the privilege of visiting Iris, an elderly lady who was dying of leukaemia. She had suffered terribly in her later years, but she was one of those people who had an inner light which suffering seemed to fuel rather than quench. As a rather naive young curate I would go to 'minister' to her, and of course I always came away having been ministered to by her. Not long before her death she was, she claimed, visited by her deceased mother who came to reassure her and told her about the preparations being made for her arrival in heaven. When she talked of these visits, it was as if she had peeped into heaven itself. Those of us who have been with the dying have probably known of a number of people who have had this experience.

And what are we to make of it? Is it psychological, something to do with the stress of dying? Is it a place-memory, or a demon in disguise? Is it an unquiet spirit? Well, in the case of Iris none of these answers are satisfactory, and the only answer I am satisfied with is the notion that at certain crisis times, like death, the departed are permitted to come as encouragers, because, after all, they are part of that great cloud of witnesses who surround us.

Although this sort of experience is common at or near the time of death, there are other testimonies to this happening at other times. For example, there is that curious story in *Ring of Truth* where J. B. Phillips has an experience of meeting the spirit of C. S. Lewis:

> Many of us who believe in what is technically known as the Communion of Saints, must have experienced the sense of nearness, for a fairly short time, of those who we love soon after they have died . . . The late C. S. Lewis, whom I did not know very well and had only seen in the flesh once, but with whom I had corresponded a fair amount, gave me an unusual experience. A few days after his death, while I was watching television, he 'appeared' sitting in a chair within a few feet of me, and spoke a few words which were particularly relevant to the circumstances through which I was passing.[5]

There are of course in the Catholic tradition numerous examples of Mary and other saints appearing and giving messages. In recent years there has been a great deal of interest in the messages apparently given by Mary to the children at Medjugorje in Yugoslavia. It is impossible to know how to judge these appearances, but there does seem to be sufficient evidence to suggest that God, under certain circumstances, does permit a soul to visit this world for the purpose of communicating an important message.

HEALING THE HURT

Whether we like it or not, experiences of hauntings and encounters with the dead are fairly common, and those of us who are part of the Church of Jesus Christ, who is the glorious conqueror of death, are responsible for trying to understand these things. Those who have some experience of haunting are often left feeling hurt. They may be frightened, confused, even feel guilty or suspect that they have some unsociable 'bug' that will make them distinctly unpopular in Christian circles. We will need to seek God for discernment and understanding to enable us to search for the right cause of the phenomenon. If the cause is psychological, then the person will need sensitive counselling to disentangle fact from fantasy, to do the letting-go work, and to deal with the pressing problem that is giving rise to these hallucinations.

Where the cause is due to some psychic ability to see into areas which are not permitted and where there is that ability to engage the place-memory phenomenon, then I would recommend that the person receive some simple cleansing and freeing prayer. In this sort of prayer I would ask them to repent of whatever psychic ability they have. I would then cut them free in Jesus' name from the effects of this ability and ask the Spirit of God to cleanse and renew them and heal any damage done. This is often quite a simple exercise, although it should be said that when people have had deep involvement in these things the process can be a long one.

In the case of the place-memory phenomenon, there may need to be some prayers said in the area of the ghost manifestation. For one reason or another there is an appearance, and even if it is a type of 'photo', it is still a presence which does not belong in this world. It still records perhaps a hurt from the past that has left its mark and may have power and influence on the living. It may not be scientific, but the fact is that people are affected by 'atmospheres', sometimes quite powerfully. In such a case, prayer for healing a hurt from the past would be appropriate.

In my experience, when the lives of those who have had psychic ability come under the lordship of Jesus and the influence of the Holy Spirit, this ability becomes sanctified and they are the people who are very open to the more intuitive gifts of visions, pictures, words of knowledge, etc.

Where we discern that the haunting has a demonic origin, then clearly deliverance ministry is appropriate and necessary, and deliverance prayers should be said by those experienced in that field.

Where the apparition is discerned as being actually the soul of the departed, then we do clearly need to discover the reason for the presence of this soul. He or she may be there in a type of angel-messenger ministry for some reason, expressly permitted by God to speak to the living. I am well aware that we are on somewhat shaky ground here, but I think that the way to test these things is to judge by their fruits. For example, take the case of the appearances at Medjugorje: there are many Christians, evangelicals included, who have flocked to this village, to be present in the village church when Mary appears to the children there. The children claim that Mary speaks an evangelical message of repentance and exhorts her listeners to proclaim Jesus to a needy world.

If the fruit of this is that a cult of Medjugorje is founded and that Marian devotion replaces devotion of Jesus, then I would question the source of the visions. If however; as seems to be the case at the moment, the fruit of the visions is a revival of faith in Jesus in a highly secular country, then I will probably want to say that God is always bigger than the little box we want to put him in, and if he chooses to bless people through this type of phenomenon, who are we to argue? It could be a case of 'what God has cleansed, do not call common'.

One regular experience of those who experience renewal is to find that God, from time to time, has to lower a sheet before us of things that we had hitherto written off as unsound, 'unblessable', useless to God, and we have to repent of the judgements we have made, and open our hearts to a new channel of God's blessing. Thus you might get someone from a house church receiving blessing through experiencing a Rite A communion service, or an evangelical discovering a new depth of prayer through the rosary or benediction. And I for one want to be open to receiving blessings from the Lord, from wherever he chooses. Having said all this, we cannot abdicate our responsibility to weigh and discern and to seek the truth in all things. In these days we urgently need the Spirit of truth that he may lead us into all truth, and note, the discovery of truth is not to lead us into legalism, but to set us free.

Finally, a haunting may be due to the presence of the unquiet dead, and it is to this subject that we turn in the next chapter and we shall find that there is a close connection here between hauntings and hurtings – hurt not only in the living but also in the dead.

And what of my night-time visitor? Just who or what was he? In this chapter I have presented the possible options and, as I said at the beginning, my conviction for many years was that he was a demon impersonation. I am now not convinced of that understanding, and I am now really too far away from that experience to come to an accurate conclusion. If it was the soul of some man who was a Quaker, a soul still trapped in this world, then I do pray that he will be released and that God will take his soul. How all this happens is the subject of our next chapter.

5

Healings and Requiems

> In this kind of general prayer, therefore, 'for the faithful departed', I conceive myself to be clearly justified, both by the earliest antiquity, by the Church of England, and by the Lord's Prayer. (John Wesley[1])

The word 'requiem', according to the dictionary, means 'a service, with or without music, for the dead'. By this definition it could equally apply to an ordinary funeral service or a special occasion including the Eucharist. I remember taking a funeral service at the crematorium in Bolton when I was a curate. As we came to the section in the service for prayers before the final committal of the body for cremation, I asked for a time of quiet. Then I said something like the following: 'As we begin our prayers for Jack, it might just be that some of us are thinking, "If only I had known when he was going to die, I would have said this or that to him." Or perhaps some of you would have done some special service or act of love for him. But because he has died you may be feeling that you are stuck with unsaid words or unfulfilled deeds. Well, through Jesus, you have an opportunity to offer Jack your words and deeds. So in the silence, open your heart to Jesus and through him say those words you wanted to say, give those deeds you wanted to do. Let Jesus take your gifts and reach out in eternity and touch Jack with them, because God is the God of the living, both in this world and the next.'

When the service was over, a number of people came up to

me and said that they followed my advice and found that, as
they silently prayed, they felt that they had been healed of such
things as migraine, arthritis and, in one case, angina. Their
simple act of requiem had brought a measure of healing to
their lives. This is not too hard for us to accept, and many
ministers could testify to similar happenings. It could be said
that the mourners were enabled through prayer to redress or
come to terms with their relationship with the deceased and
ask forgiveness, and the release which follows often results in
physical benefits. This testifies to the fact that we are a unity
of mind, emotions and body. To receive blessing in one area
of our lives cannot but touch upon the other aspects also. Of
course the funeral service is also the time when we can commend the departing soul to continue its journey fortified by
God's keeping love and power. Incidentally, when we are not
certain, or even if we know that the deceased was not a committed Christian and born again of the Holy Spirit, it is still incum-
bent upon us to be charitable towards them as we commend
them to the issues of eternity. Therefore an early conclusion
here is that we can all be involved in requiem healing to some
degree, simply by caring for the departed and underlining our
respect and love for them in the funeral service we attend.

However, the issue of requiem healing has been taken much
further to incorporate ideas such as releasing the departed from
a kind of purgatory in order to enter heaven, the healing of
the living from ills which were common to the departed, the
recognising of forgotten lives such as aborted and still-born
babies along with miscarried pregnancies and the breaking of
generational sins and curses which have come down the family
tree to afflict the living. Perhaps the foremost practitioner of
this developed approach to requiem is Dr Kenneth McAll.

For the purpose of this book we shall be looking at Dr
McAll's approach to requiem healing and examining how they
compare with our studies so far.[2] Ken McAll comes from a
family of evangelical and non-conformist missionaries to China.

His mother's family were members of the London Missionary Society and his father's background was that of Congregational preachers. Indeed, one of his relatives founded what is today the Protestant Evangelical Mission Church in France. He remembers as a child having family prayers and reading *Daily Light*. As a missionary in China himself, he was challenged by the way an itinerant Chinese woman preacher delivered a man of demonic power in the name of Jesus. This brought the whole issue of possession to his attention. His studies, which included a degree of psychiatry, began to focus upon the relationship between the possessed mind and the resultant effect upon the body. He also noticed that some patients seemed to act out the illnesses which were known to afflict their deceased relatives. In one case early on in his ministry he approached the suffragan Bishop of Ludlow, the Rt Revd Parkinson, for advice about a family he was seeking to help. He was quite surprised when the Bishop suggested the holding of the requiem Eucharist for the deceased. He recalls that on the Monday when the Eucharist was held his patient, who was in a padded cell in a London hospital, was healed. At the same time his patient's aunt, who was in a mental hospital in north Wales, was also healed. The actual diagnosis of his patient in London was that of hallucinogenic schizophrenia. Apparently she had an urge to gouge out the eyes of people.[3] It seemed that the holding of a requiem Eucharist for a deceased relative who had similarly exhibited a form of schizophrenia resulted in the healing of such illness amongst the living. This experience was formative for Dr McAll, who now works almost always through the vehicle of the Eucharist, which he suggests is the most powerful context for healing, both for the living and the departed.

THE POSSESSION SYNDROME

The possession states which McAll first noticed in China, he found also in the United Kingdom. However, he was to define this term more precisely and so he suggested three forms of the possession syndrome: that of the living to the living, the living to the dead, and the living to the occult.

1. Possession: the living to the living

We are all familiar with stories of people being in bondage to another person's will. The cases of the possessive parent who dominates the child either by sheer will power or by smother love are well documented. Leanne Payne, in her book *The Broken Image*, suggests that one of the reasons for emerging homosexual behaviour in people is in response to this wrong kind of parenting. Freedom and healing came when the domination was confronted and broken, and when, through the love of Jesus, the 'injured' party was enabled to forgive their parent and choose to live more freely in God.[4] In *Healing the Family Tree* Dr McAll tells the story of Ruth, the dominant mother of her son Rufus. Rufus was eight years old when his father died, and from then on he had felt that his life was completely ordered by his mother. His career and even choice of wife were all his mother's choice. His wife was in a sanatorium suffering from tuberculosis and Rufus was a schizophrenic, confined to a mental hospital. The mother, on being challenged to face up to her domination of her son was at first angry and stormed out of the consulting room. However, later on whilst in church, God challenged her to repent and to cut the umbilical cord to Rufus, her youngest child. She fell to her knees and said: 'If this is true, Lord, I will do it now.' In McAll's own words:

> On this fateful Thursday afternoon, Rufus had felt a sudden surge of release. He wrote immediately to his mother, telling her that 'he felt he was himself again' and that he had asked

the hospital for permission to spend the next weekend with his brother. Rufus was wholly cured. His wife also had felt unusually well on the same day and, after various tests had proved negative, was discharged from the sanatorium . . . Twenty years later, Rufus and his wife are still fit and well.[5]

This form of healing and deliverance does not present any real problems to most of us. The ministry of inner healing has been adopted by many Christians over the last twenty years. The problems begin to emerge when the one who has exercised such domination over another is dead and apparently beyond our reach.

2. Possession: the living to the dead

This is by far the most controversial aspect of Dr McAll's teaching on possession. He contends that the illnesses and disturbances, be they 'ghosts' or 'voices in the mind', which the living suffer are due to the unquiet dead. He says that those who were unprepared for death

. . . can see that they are out of the body but do not know where they are. Because they are not committed and haven't had a funeral service, they are still earthbound. Therefore they are wandering and so look for family members through whom they can register their presence.[6]

Dr McAll substantiates his belief with an impressive number of recorded case-histories. Therefore his response to need is to construct a family tree of the patient and see if there are any similarities in the behaviour of the living one who is distressed to the known behaviour of the deceased. Secondly, he would look for any cases of unprepared death in the family line. It seems that the most common category for the latter is that of abortion, spontaneous or otherwise. Once the departed relative has been identified, then a Eucharist is held where the dead are specifically named and where the need for forgiveness for them or the living is pronounced. In cases of anorexia nervosa, where the deceased person is so named, Dr McAll cites an 85 per cent success rate.

Whilst the evidence of healing is very substantial, his thesis contains some serious questions for us. First of all, is it true that it is actually the dead who are exercising some hold over the living? Could it not be demonic spirits at work or the projection of the troubled person who gives external reality to his or her inward hurt of sins? Dr McAll is well aware of these possibilities, as we shall see in the next section.

However, it is a basic evangelical conviction that the dead are held in some place awaiting the judgement of God, whether this is paradise or hades. Dr McAll suggests that the dead do go to a place like purgatory where they need to undergo necessary cleansing and freeing from any unfinished business. The requiem ministry has the effect of releasing the trapped soul and enabling it to go on its way to its journey's end in heaven. We have seen that there are some grounds for this as far as the Christian dead are concerned. The real difficulty comes when Dr McAll says that such freeing and releasing into heaven is also true for the unsaved or uncommitted dead. Is this salvation after death? Dr McAll refers to those who are somehow trapped as 'lost souls' and distinguishes between them and those who have damned themselves in whatever way such an action may be possible.[7] He is not very clear about what this action is, but he nonetheless says that those who have died without commitment to Christ do find release through a requiem Eucharist and find their way to God. Whilst he wants to resist going down the road to universalism he emphasises that God is still gracious after death as well as before. I think that this is a necessary challenge to evangelicals who paint a picture of a God whose love runs out for the lost when they die.

However, whilst Dr McAll (quoting William Barclay), says that the word 'judgement' in the New Testament implies discipline rather than punishment, he cannot escape the fact that Scripture does teach that, without a commitment to Christ, death brings a prospect of spending eternity without enjoying the fellowship of God.[8] This is not to deny or undermine the healing which has come to his patients, but there is a great need to be cautious when making statements about the deceased now entering heaven. In the final analysis such statements cannot be verified and only hold importance for the individual concerned. Dr McAll, as well as some of his patients, reports seeing in a visionary way the deceased sharing in the Eucharist and going up into a great light. For example, during one such requiem he was puzzled to see a young airman called Keith, still in uniform, reluctantly enter the church and, after reflecting upon the message of the Eucharist, going up into a great light and looking very peaceful. During a meal afterwards he spoke to the mother who had requested this ministry for her eighteen-year-old son who was addicted to drugs. He asked her who Keith was. She was very agitated by this question and revealed that she had previously married an eighteen-year-old called Keith, who had been shot down over the Baltic ocean three months after their marriage. Only her husband knew of this; none of her children had been informed. Interestingly enough, the son had been going to the Baltic coast to indulge his drug-taking. He was healed as a result of this service and no longer resorted to the habit.[9]

However, it is just this kind of visionary link[10] which gives rise to the question whether this is not spiritualism in another guise. Dr McAll is very specific when he says that this form of requiem healing is talking to the Lord about the dead and not talking to the dead. He never encourages the living to seek contact with the dead. In fact he believes that spiritualism is a great evil and opens the door to spiritual forces that bring harm to the living as well as the dead. We have a lot of biblical evidence for people speaking about their dead to the Lord. Daniel prays to God about the sins of their fathers who had caused their predicament in captivity (Dan. 9:16). The psalmist prays to God that he will not hold the sins of his fathers against him (Ps. 79:8). It could be said that the whole institution of the Day of Atonement hinged upon remembering the ill effects of the ministry of Aaron's sons, Nadab and Abihu (Num. 3:4; Lev. 16:1ff). The great prayer of the Levitical priests in Nehemiah is a conversation with God about the lives of Abraham and Moses and the disobedience of the rulers who came after them (Neh. 9). Also Paul, then writing to Timothy, speaks of the apparently deceased Onesiphorus, that God would be merciful to him on the day of Judgement (1 Tim. 1:16–18). On this evidence then we cannot say that requiem healing is spiritualism; in fact it is in keeping with the practice of both the Old and New Testament saints.

Some have questioned the validity of this form of healing because they do not believe that the living can be affected by the dead. However, there is evidence for this in the Bible itself. There are a number of prayers and sacrifices which deal with the need for deliverance from the sins of the fathers.[11] We have already referred to the subject of sins and curses being visited upon the generations, and surely in order to break this there is the need to ask God for release and forgiveness for the sins of our dead relatives.[12] I think it is also implicit in the death of Christ that when the Bible says that he died not only for our sins but for the sins of the whole world, this means not only that there is provision for all to be saved but that there is provision for all to be delivered from the sinful effects of those who have harmed us. Jesus offers us a salvation which leads to healing and wholeness.

In the process of his work Dr McAll has discovered that one of the reasons why some people are disturbed is due to abortion, stillbirth or miscarriage that has happened within the family. The documentation for mothers suffering with guilt long after they have had an abortion is well recorded. Dr McAll maintains that in all these cases it is a real life that has been lost and which feels rejected, and being nameless it does not feel part of the family to which it belongs. The requiem offers a chance to say sorry to such a baby (through the person of Jesus Christ) and then to name their child. In cases where the sex of the child is not known, then it is advised that the parents pray about this and proceed as they feel led. The release for the parents is often powerful and there can be dramatic healings also. Dr McAll says that this form of requiem has the effect of recognising, loving and accepting the forgotten or lost life. The following is a case-history from my own involvement in requiem healing:

Frank was concerned for his 26-year-old son Bob who was living the life of a homosexual transvestite. Frank was a committed Christian and an elder in his local independent evangelical church. His son had left some years before to train as a chef. He had not really had a close relationship with his father for some years. At the time when Frank requested help, his wife had been dead for about six years. Bob had announced to his father that he was thinking of going to America with his boy-friend. In his homosexual relationship Bob exercised the female role. Frank feared he would lose contact with his son alto-gether, and it was this which prompted him to seek help. Frank was quite an outspoken critic of his son's way of life, but he did love his son even though he did not show his affection adequately as far as his son was concerned.

When I met with Frank to discuss how to pray for his son, I asked him to give me a full account of the members of his family and anything which would throw further light on Bob's behaviour. Frank told me that his son was a twin and that at the time of his birth it was discovered that the other child, a female, had died some time earlier during the pregnancy. I shared two thoughts with Frank in the light of this information. First, had he acknowledged his daughter, named her in the presence of God and commended her to the Lord Jesus? Secondly, I asked him to consider the fact that during Bob's earliest moments of life he was intimately related and connected to his sister, and that at some time during the relationship, which would include not only physical but also emotional dimensions, the female life he had known from conception had gone without warning and preparation. Surely this was bound to affect Bob at some level.

Frank went away to consider and pray about this and we met a week later. He told me that he had had a most moving experience of God's compassion and healing. Whilst reflecting upon the fact that he had a daughter who would now be 26 years old and living in the presence of God and with whom he would one day be reunited in fellowship through Jesus, he broke down and wept. He realised that he had ignored, discounted as nothing, his own daughter who was made in the image of God. The memory also came back to him that he and his wife had always wanted a daughter of their own and, if they had, they would have called her Mary, after his own wife. So, as an act of faith, he had repented of disowning his daughter and gave her the name of 'Mary' and entrusted her to God. Frank said that although he had found the whole experience traumatic, he did feel that he had received an inner release that he had not known before. Within a day or so Bob telephoned to say that he was no longer going to America. He went on to say that earlier that day he had been sitting in his flat preparing to leave when the door opened, or so he thought. But when he turned round he could see nobody, although he was sure he had felt someone come into the room. Then he felt that someone spoke the name 'Mary' in his ear and he began to cry for no apparent reason. His crying, he later said, was a kind of release because from that moment he knew he was no longer homosexual. He cancelled his plans to go to America and eventually returned home to see his father.

Father and son were enabled to talk about their differences and find reconciliation. His father explained what we had shared, because he had not been told that he was a twin. It seems that Bob's sexuality had been confused because, after a time of complete harmony in the womb alongside his sister, when she had died something in Bob continued to look for his sister. It was only when his sister Mary had been recognised and named, that Bob, who was at least two hundred miles away at the time, received his healing. Frank found that he could 'step down' from his dominant approach to his family and open himself up much more to loving and being loved. He now enjoys his life as father and grandfather, and Bob later came to a real faith in Jesus Christ.

In these days of more abortions this kind of healing is needed more and more. I am quite sure that such a dispatching of innocent lives leaves its mark of disquiet and dis-ease not only upon the lives of those who make such decisions but also upon the hospitals which carry out such operations. I have been in conversation with a number of doctors and nurses who report that such hospitals seem to have more than their fair share of mismanaged operations (in other departments) and often seem to carry a depressive atmosphere – so much so that many of the staff prefer to work elsewhere. In several of these places some of the Christians have begun to pray for the aborted lives and ask God's forgiveness. They report an improvement in working relationships and results as a consequence.

We should not underestimate the value of naming such children before God. In doing so we are recognising that they are real people who have a true life even though they did not enjoy a proper birth and life. Consider the fact that we name our children at baptism and pray over them and commit them to God's keeping care. Such an act is meant to bond the child to Christ, his church and also the child's family in faith. Names are very powerful factors in a life. Zechariah was struck dumb when he argued with God about the naming of his son John, known as the Baptist. Neither should we be in doubt that these children are real, even though they were aborted or miscarried. After all, Jeremiah received his prophetic call in his mother's womb (Jer. 1:4–5); the unborn John the Baptist, upon hearing his mother Elizabeth speaking of the Christ to be born of Mary, responds with his own witness of joy and is promptly filled with the Holy Spirit (Luke 1:39–45). Esau and Jacob are engaged in a struggle for supremacy within their mother's womb; they 'fell out' before they 'came out' (Gen. 25:21–6). And if this were not enough to convince us, the Psalmist speaks of his formation within his mother as being under the daily super-vision of God who sees and nourishes the life within (Ps. 139:13–16).

Whether or not we can substantiate accounts of these 'forgot-ten' children being released and going on to heaven in some way, requiem healing is nonetheless a service we must render them, as well as those who lost them, if we are to cherish life from God's perspective.

3. Possession: the living to the occult

Before examining the requiem service itself we must give some consideration to the suggestion that we may not be dealing with the dead but the demonic. It is quite probable that the sources which supply family information at spiritualist seances and the likes are not the dead relatives but demonic forces impersonat-ing the dead in order to deceive and ensnare the living. Raphael Gasson, in his book *The Challenging Counterfeit*,[13] tells of a time when he challenged the alleged spirits of his dead ances-tors who were his 'spirit guides', for he was an accomplished medium. He was rudely awakened to the fact that these spirits were in fact demonic and that he needed deliverance from them in order properly to walk with God. For a more complete survey of the occult world and directions for bringing deliver-ance to such people, see my book entitled *The Occult: Deliver-ance from Evil*.[14] Dr McAll is well aware of the possibility of the demonic and so suggests that as a matter of course, with any request for healing, a careful study is made before engaging in ministry. This would include a full medical investigation, as some forms of alleged demonic activity may in fact be depressive psychosis, schizophrenia or the projections of the troubled mind. This is not to rule out the fact that given such medical problems there can still be the influence of the demonic as well. Dr McAll says that the test for whether or not there is demonic presence is in the patient's response to prayer and to the Eucharist. Even with the offering of silent prayers there can be an erratic response within the patient and this is a good clue to the need for deliverance from the demonic.

Often there will be a need to break demonic heredity in the family. Some years ago I was asked to help a member of a church who was suffering from attacks of violence and rage out of all proportion to his circumstances. Stephen reported having involuntary trances and hearing voices, at the same time he always felt as if someone was placing his hand upon his head. He had received a lot of prayer counselling but the problems persisted. As we discussed his problems we discovered that his grandmother was a medium and that when Stephen was born she had prayed over him to receive her 'psychic gifts'. Healing and deliverance only happened after he renounced his grandmother's involvement in the occult and asked for cleansing and deliverance in the name of Jesus Christ. There were no further manifestations from this time onwards. Dr McAll cites with approval a prayer by Kurt Koch which he has found helpful-when delivering people from the bondage of the occult; 'In the name of Jesus Christ I renounce all the works of the Devil together with the occult practices of my forefathers, and I submit myself to Jesus Christ, my Lord and Saviour, both now and forever.'[15]

A further contribution to this discussion on family history and the demonic is that of 'spirits of the dead'. I am grateful to Peter Horrobin, the Director of Ellel Grange, for his comments on this subject. He suggested that sometimes the problem has been that of a demonic spirit which had a hold upon the dying person and which attached itself to the living relative at the time of death. If evil spirits can attack us through the living as in the example of the man called Legion or the abortive episode of the seven sons of Sceva, then it is equally likely that such spirits can attack us through the dying who may have been similarly demonised. This would accord to some degree with Dr McAll's assertion that when there has not been a proper Christian preparation for death and committal to God after death then the deceased becomes an easy target for demonic attack. Peter Horrobin goes on to say that the form in which such spirits attach themselves to the living is to reproduce the personality of the deceased and so bring the living into a kind of bondage to the dead. Therefore in some cases where people feel dominated by a parent even though that parent has died there may well be a need for deliverance from a spirit of domination rather than just inner healing from the effect such parents may have left upon their children. Granted there is little biblical documentation for this idea but the subject deserves a lot of further discussion. However, it only serves to underline the importance of proper preparation and prayer for the dying. It also serves us well to include some general prayer of deliverance when seeking to bring healing to any relationship between the living and the dead.

Finally, we need to touch upon the whole area of ghosts and hauntings as well as the possibility that the problem is one of projection by the sufferer. It is possible that some of the problems we feel about the dead are the projected hurts we feel inside. Very often, if we have felt guilty about the way we have treated someone who has died, we may imagine that we see them haunting our lives. Dr McAll says that very often ghosts are issues of human form that we do not want to face. He cites the example of the prudish spinster who might see in dark doorways figures of men intent upon rape because she fears her sexuality but denies this until it is projected. Ghosts may well appear as lustful figures.[16] He suggests that one way to minister to this, far from denying 'her ghosts', is to hold a Christian service for 'whatever may be there'. This allows the person to forgive whatever she cannot face and so switch her focus to Jesus and overcome her fear. Such an approach helps the person to become reconciled to that part of themselves they have been denying.

More and more Christians are coming to realise nowadays that most of the ghosts reported are not necessarily demonic but the distressed dead who have somehow become trapped upon earth. This is usually because the death of the person concerned was unplanned – as in the case of murder, death by disease or war – or there were no proper funeral rites or prayers of committal. This means that they are distressed and in need of some direction. It is up to us as Christians to declare the lordship of Christ over their presence and over their problems. Far from needing the ministry of deliverance then, what is more appropriate is some form of requiem healing. Such a service is the fulfilling of what was denied to them by virtue of their unprepared death. Most evangelicals when taking a funeral service include some form of prayers for the departed which commend them to the peace of God. It is not for us to make decisions about whether they were truly converted or not. In the final analysis only two people really know how a person stands with the Almighty, they are the individual concerned and God himself. Therefore a requiem service offers those forgotten prayers of committal which have been unsaid for however many years since they had died. Surely if we feel it proper to pray for the departed some days after their death at a funeral service, then praying for them many years after death is a crossing of the same divide.

I well remember listening to an edition of 'Woman's Hour' on Radio 4 some years ago. It dealt with the visit, the first by any pontiff, of Pope John Paul II to the site of the death camp of Auschwitz in Poland. The woman reporting on the visit said that it was a place where no bird sang nor plants grew. There the feeling of the horrific deaths of millions hung like a dark shadow over the place. However, on the very day that the Pope celebrated the Eucharist and related the death of Christ to the slaughter of millions of his fellow countrymen, the birds began to sing and the whole atmosphere changed. No doubt this is a very subjective observation, but it speaks very powerfully about the need to bring the death and resurrection of Jesus Christ to the many who have died without being remembered. This is why Dr McAll suggests that the ideal context for a requiem healing is that of the Eucharist or the breaking of bread.

REQUIEM HEALING AND THE EUCHARIST

The practice of holding services for the dead in combination with the Holy Communion is an old and well-attested practice of the Christian Church. The writings of Teresa of Avila, Thomas Aquinas, Bernard of Clairvaux and Elizabeth of Hungary all refer to the healing power of the Eucharist both for the living and for the dead. Matthew and Dennis Linn mention in their book Bernard's account of how St Malachy held a series of requiem Eucharists for his dead sister. They had not got on well for some years. One night Malachy dreamt of his sister standing at his door in need of food and refreshment. When he awoke and reflected upon his dream it occurred to him that the food she needed was the living bread of Jesus Christ. So he held a number of communion services for her until in his dreams he saw her now released from her poor state and in the blessing of God.[17] Whatever substance we wish to give to his actions and convictions we must nonetheless note that the saint also received a healing, because he at last had come to terms with his sister. We need to keep in focus that in the final event, the requiem must be for the benefit of the living.

Dr McAll advises that, apart from the minister, we need to decide who should be present at the service. Whenever possible it should include the living person in need of prayer as they can use the occasion to accept Jesus Christ's love for themselves as for their deceased family members. Other loving friends or family, who wish to pray or who are prepared to be open to the love and power of God in Jesus should be invited. He suggests beginning with informal prayer in which God the Father is asked to call out to the dead who live before him and enable them to witness the acts of love and confession which are to take place.

He divides the requiem service into four stages from this point:

1. Deliver us from evil

Using the Lord's Prayer to begin the service we ask God to free both the living and the dead from any bondage to the evil one. As the Eucharist focuses upon the blood of Christ represented by the wine, such deliverance is inviting the Lord Jesus to cleanse the blood lines of the living and the dead of all that blocks healthy life. This would include the breaking of hereditary seals and curses by casting out any evil spirits. We have already examined the subject of how demonic spirits can attach themselves to families down through the generations, and so beginning any requiem service in this manner is a way in fact of opening up all the needy areas to the lordship and power of Jesus Christ. This often helps to release more of the healing power of the Holy Spirit for the benefit of the living.

2. Forgiveness

It is vital that the living let go of any resentments, hurts or guilt that make them hold on to or be held by the departed or the demonic. Dr McAll goes further and says that in the requiem forgiveness is offered to the departed. He underlines the familiar words of the eucharistic prayer which, in speaking of the blood of Christ, says 'which was shed for you and for the sins of many'. The many are to include the living who have never received Christ's forgiveness and the departed who may never have been told of God's love for them in Jesus. He also says that the Eucharist offers a double forgiveness, as it includes an opportunity to ask the departed to forgive us. Many a mother has come to this place and, through confession to Jesus Christ, has asked forgiveness from the children whom she has aborted or whom she took no notice of because they were miscarried early in the pregnancy. Certainly when we ask for forgiveness it is like letting go of issues we have either denied or held on to for years. It can bring great relief and healing as well as lead us to the place where we can hold a better and more positive relationship with that person.

Some time ago I led a group of street evangelists in a biblical meditation where they were encouraged to imagine themselves walking down a sort of Emmaus road. They were to choose any road they knew and then after seeing themselves walking along it, Jesus would come and join them. Here they were to share with him any issue that concerned them and then listen to what the Lord would give them in exchange. At an appropriate moment they were to go and share with another what the Lord had said to them. Almost a year later I was sitting in the team lounge at the Spring Harvest event in Minehead when one of these evangelists came up to me and shared what the exercise had meant to her. As soon as she closed her eyes she found herself in a wooded clearing near a town she knew very well. In the clearing she found Jesus and with him was a very young and playful boy. As she looked Jesus said to her, 'This is your son R —, I want you to know that he is in my care but you can play with him for a few moments before I take him home with me.' The young boy duly ran to her and she held him in her arms and loved him and wept. The woman went on to tell me that she had had an abortion some years ago and had never felt free enough to tell anyone, and the guilt had left a scar on her emotions which prevented her from really entering into all that the Lord had for her. But now she felt so full of joy because Jesus had her son and he was growing up with the angels. She said that she had been forgiven and was free to go forward with God for the first time in years.

3. The offering

Dr McAll places great importance upon this moment because it is a sharing and a witnessing to the offering of Christ's death and resurrection: 'Whenever you eat this bread and drink this cup, you proclaim the Lord's death until he comes' (1 Cor. 11:26). During this part of the service the people concerned are encouraged to place their family trees or the written names of people for whom they are specifically praying or even gifts and tokens of love for the departed on the table along with the gifts of bread and wine. This is a good suggestion because it helps us to see our giving in the light of the gift of the son of God for us all. It is an opportunity to name the individuals for whom we have come to pray. In doing so we recognise their right to live and give dignity to their person, especially if this was denied to them in their death. It is at moments like this that death wishes are broken in those suffering from anorexia nervosa. They are given space at the requiem to offer love and forgiveness to the one they miss so much, and it is a way of saying goodbye: 'You are now in your rightful place in my heart.' Many taking part at this point in the requiem report seeing their deceased relatives entering into the joy and peace of Christ. These are purely personal visions and should be kept as such, but it is interesting to know that they do not lead to attempts to hold on to the dead or to communicate with them afterwards. The whole point about requiem is that the living and deceased have come to terms with each other through Christ, and so there can be a letting go of the dead into the hands of God.

4. *The blessing*

Here we see the focus shifting from the needs of the dead on to those of the living. It is an opportunity to lay hands on them and pray silently or otherwise for them to receive whatever healing God wishes to give them. It is also an opportunity for anointing and for the signing of the cross. Here we can turn fully to Jesus and offer ourselves for his service now that we have been released and renewed. We can move on from being bound in an unhealthy way to the past and go forward in the power of the Holy Spirit. As the final words from the Rite A of the Eucharist in *The Alternative Service Book* exhort us, we are to:

Minister: Go in peace to love and serve the Lord.
People: In the name of Christ, Amen!

Before asking ourselves what differences requiem healing can make to our Christian lives we must see if a model for this kind of ministry can be found in the Bible. I believe that Jesus offers just such a model and he demonstrates it when he found friends in a cemetery.

Jesus the Model for Requiems

> Jesus called in a loud voice: 'Lazarus, come out!' The dead
> man came out . . . Jesus said to them: 'Take off the grave
> clothes and let him go.'   (John 11:43–4)

The purpose of this chapter is to offer a biblical outline for an
approach to requiem healing. We have discussed in some depth
the whole issue of relationships between the living and the dead
and reviewed a particular approach to requiem ministry. Now
we need to find a way in which we can benefit from this ministry
whilst retaining our commitment to the word of God. In the
beautiful story of Lazarus being raised from the dead, we find
that Jesus' healing touch gives life to the mourners as well as
to the departed. Jesus' ministry to the grieving family offers us
three principles which we can incorporate as we engage in the
need for requiem healing. They are as follows:

> listening to the wounds;
> ministering to the departed;
> restoring the relationship.

LISTENING TO THE WOUNDS

When Martha and Mary hear that Jesus is outside they rush to
him and share their hurt. They both give a voice to their pain
and anger when they say, 'Lord, if only you had been here,
my brother would not have died.' They seem to imply that

Lazarus shouldn't be dead and that if Jesus had been present he could have healed him and prevented this. Perhaps this is a clue to how unprepared they were for the death of their brother. Jesus, upon hearing their story and seeing their distress, is moved deeply and weeps himself. What a tremendous contrast this is; he who is the Resurrection and the Life stands by a tomb and weeps. This should encourage us to share our hurt feelings with Jesus about our departed. It is good to know that his resurrection life and power does not hush our crying. Similarly, at funerals and requiems, Jesus gives us space to share with him our hurt about the departed. And he listens to our wounds. It is also a place to share our hopes for the departed. Martha and Mary both looked forward to seeing Lazarus again on the day of Resurrection. Then they would see him free of his ills and in full vigour of life. A requiem gives us an opportunity also to share our hope that our departed will be healed of their ills and enjoy the kingdom life of God in eternity. The following is a summary of some of the wounds that we might be carrying either about or from the departed.

1. Unprepared deaths
Here we are thinking primarily of those who had little or no opportunity to prepare their souls for death and leaving their families and friends. These deaths are due to such things as accidents, acts of violence, as in war or murder, unforseen illnesses and suicide. Very often the living can still be suffering from the shock or guilt of their sudden removal.

I remember praying with a friend whose father had died quite suddenly when he was only seven years old. Three months later his mother committed suicide and so he was brought up by a distant aunt. Years later he still had feelings of being abandoned and felt overcome by the temptation to give up on life when it became difficult. We prayed for his parents, and suddenly a 'picture' forcibly came to his mind of his father in the hospital in which he died. Jack was actually out of the room when his father died, but in this picture he saw Jesus help him climb on to the bed with his father. His father hugged him and said how sorry he was to be dying as he felt he had not given enough love and affection to Jack. Jack became very emotional and told his father that he had always thought he had died in order to get away from him. Now he knew his father loved him and he thanked Jesus for giving him this insight. After this he found that he had a lot more inner strength in his Christian life and more stability in times of crisis. This experience also became the springboard by which he could appreciate his mother more completely and accept her death, tragic as it was. Jesus had brought Jack to a place where he listened to his wounds.

2. The unquiet dead

These are spirits of the departed, who have been unable to find their proper place of rest and seek to bring this to the notice of the living. They can be members of our own family from past generations or people who are attached to the place of their death or suffering. Here we need to do our homework, and, provided we are satisfied that such happenings are not demonic in origin and are sure of the identity of the departed, we need to bring their wound to Christ. We speak on their behalf rather than just our own.

3. The forgotten dead

Here we are reowning as ours and God's those lives which were aborted or lost through miscarriage. There is also an opportunity for the ones responsible for abortion to repent and receive forgiveness and be released from the effects of the guilt which they have been carrying. There can be space to apologise through Christ to our children for rejecting them and not recognising them as ours, made equally in the image of God as ourselves. It can be a very liberating thing to know that the children we forgot have not been forgotten by God and that in due time we shall all be together with the Lord.

4. The wounds of the dead

Here we are dealing with the sins, curses or afflictions which have come down within the generations of the family. There may be a need to break the bondage of evil spirits from our families in order that the living may go free. We may need to repent on behalf of our ancestors. This is perfectly in order when we consider that the great saints of the Old Testament often prayed for the sins of the nation and their forefathers. People like Ezra, Jeremiah and Daniel often prayed, 'O Lord forgive us for we have sinned'. We already know that they had not rebelled in the way that the nation had, but they still included themselves and identified themselves as being equally responsible before God. Also, the Lord's Prayer reminds us that we need to forgive others their trespasses against us in order for God to forgive ours. This passage needs to be understood in two basic ways. First, it refers to the way in which we may be holding on to bitterness and grievances due to how folk have sinned towards us and hurt us. It is as if our lives are full of the consequences of unforgiveness and God cannot find room to give us his healing. Those whom we need to forgive can be the dead just as much as the living. When we let go of the issues we have been nursing and keeping alive within our hearts, then, and only then, do we find that now we have space to be more open to God and enjoy his forgiveness and blessing.

A second approach to this passage is that of bringing the sins of our departed dead to Christ, asking his forgiveness in order that the consequences of these ancestral sins which have influenced the living may be broken and removed. Where there has been former involvement in the occult there is often a history of mental and emotional stress in the descendants. Prayers of deliverance, which can only come when forgiveness has been received, have often resulted in the hurting family being delivered of demonic influence and real healing taking place.

. Sometimes, when there has been deep shock or hurt to the family, this can have far-reaching effects upon succeeding generations. I remember, some years ago now, being asked to pray for a person because he was afraid that the family 'curse' was going to catch up with him. He described how the men in his family had had an almost continuous history of mental illness which afflicted them around their fortieth year. Through prayer and sharing it came to our knowledge that almost a hundred years earlier one of his great-grandmothers, when pregnant, had witnessed a brutal stabbing. She was so shocked by the event that she went into labour and gave birth to a baby boy. Apparently the mother was in her early forties when this happened. In subsequent prayers and ministry, intercessions were offered for the moment when mother and son were in shock, with the request that the effects of this experience be removed from the rest of the family. Not long after this time, both the person's father and grandfather improved so much that they were discharged from the mental hospitals where they had been. He, himself, is happily married and enjoying life in his forties.

It is certainly true that we shall not be judged by the sins of our forebears but, as the word 'atonement' implies, we may need to have the effect of such sins or curses lifted from us. Thank God, he has provided a place for us at Calvary where we can come in faith and offer any sins and know they will be removed, because Jesus died not only for our sins but for the sins of the whole world (1 John 2:2). Therefore we join with Jesus when we listen to the wounds that the living may be carrying about their dead and, having listened, the next step is to engage in the appropriate ministry.

MINISTERING TO THE DEPARTED

Having been deeply moved by the love and pain he saw at
Lazarus' graveside, Jesus then turns his attention from the
living to the dead and says, 'Take away the stone' (John 11:38).
Martha immediately reminds Jesus of the finality and fruits of
death; her brother's body had been interred for four days and
the decomposition would be quite marked. Yet the subject of
death is no barrier to the power of Jesus Christ; he enters in
where we fear to tread. The removing of the stone tells us that
there is no blockage of access for Jesus: here he enters the
realms of the dead long before he went and preached to the
imprisoned spirits in Hades (1 Pet. 3:19; 4:6). Another important factor is that Jesus goes to the place of death and brings
his healing. This was to prove so vital and true for his own
death, soon to follow. Therefore, we can go with Jesus to the
place of death, not necessarily the actual grave, but by faith
into the time, the issues as well as the place, of death which
we are considering in our request for requiem healing. Because
Jesus is the Resurrection and the Life, the most suitable context
for this ministry, though by no means the only one, is that of
the communion service.

There are a number of reasons for the appropriateness and
the power of such prayer within the communion service itself.
At the heart of the Eucharist are the twin issues of proclamation
and remembrance. Paul says that participation in the Lord's
supper is a way of 'proclaiming the Lord's death until he comes'
(1 Cor. 11:26). So the communion becomes a visual demon-
stration of Christ's death and resurrection to all. This theme is
picked up in the liturgy of both the Anglican and Roman
Catholic rites. The Proper Preface to the Sanctus says: 'Therefore with angels and archangels and all the company of heaven,
we proclaim your great and glorious name . . .'[1] Here the living
and departed, alike and together, proclaim – to all who will
hear – the greatness and the majesty of the Lord Jesus Christ.

The proclaiming of the name of Christ moves on to proclaiming 'his mighty resurrection and glorious ascension'.[2] We can complete this idea of proclamation by looking to the words of Paul in Ephesians where he says that, through the Church, the manifold wisdom of God will be made known to the rulers and authorities in the heavenly realms (Eph. 3:10). The Eucharist is one of these moments when the Church declares together with the heavenly host, to all the powers and authorities, the wisdom and the power of the cross.

Also at the core of the Eucharist is the value of remembrance. Jesus encourages us to take part in this celebratory meal in remembrance of him. So we remember a particular death at this table of the new covenant. Because we are allowed to reach back and touch the death of Christ, even so, through him, we can touch those deaths of our family which are significant for us. We can say to the deaths that have touched us deeply that here is another death, more powerful in its effect than theirs. Therefore the healing effects of Christ's death can overcome whatever ills or hurts these others may have brought. In remembering our departed, we can say that the death of Christ, and the shedding of his precious blood, was not only for the forgiveness of our sins but for their sins, for the sins of the many. So we identify ourselves with the healing of the cross and proclaim it to be more powerful in its effects than any issue which has hurt us from our departed dead. We can also proclaim that such healing was offered for them too and leave the consequences of such witness to the faithful working of the Holy Spirit.

To summarise, we can say that the Holy Communion is the best context for requiem ministry because:

it proclaims the power of Christ's death;
it proclaims God's offer of salvation;
it proclaims deliverance from demonic power (see Col. 2:15);
it proclaims God's offer of forgiveness for all.

RESTORING THE RELATIONSHIP

After Jesus had called to him, Lazarus came out from the tomb, with all the trappings of death upon him. So Jesus instructs his friends to take off the grave clothes and let him go. It wasn't enough to bring him back to the world of the living; he needed to be given back his family.

This is always the touchstone of whether requiem ministry has been properly completed. The living come to a place where they have a proper relationship with their dead. In the case of Lazarus it was a restoring to life and a renewal of his place alongside his sisters in his home. Whilst we cannot usually expect a rising from the dead, we can hope for a renewal in the way the living will now be able to relate to their dead relatives. The Lazarus story tells us, however, that God does want to restore a true and proper relationship between us and our departed. For example, if we are asking God to forgive us for forgetting or treating as nought a miscarried life or an aborted life, then in recognising the dignity of that person we have brought ourselves back into a proper relationship with them. We hold them in our hearts and, if they are already in God's kingdom care, then we have God's word to assure us that on the last day we shall be together with the Lord forever (1 Thes. 4:16–18). If we have been remembering those who were ill-treated, killed violently or who carried great hurts, then in requiem we are saying that we recognise their right to life and that Jesus' offer of healing was equally for them. As to the consequences for their life in eternity resulting from this action, it is not for us to say. We offer them to God and accept that they are ours, they are part of our family, and we can go on into our future safe in the knowledge that we have been released from any hold or effect that they may have had upon us. Requiem healing helps to create, by the grace of God, an appropriate relationship with our departed and, because of this, the departed are much freer to go on into what God has for them.

Requiem Healing and Pastoral Care

If we adopt the views that we have expressed in this book, what difference does it make to our walk with God and the way we care for his people? Both of us have been involved in pastoral work for many years, and we both share the same concern that what we write should not be theory for textbook study, but should be something that can be worked out in life. In this chapter we suggest a number of ways of working it out.

GIVING PEOPLE PERMISSION TO LOVE THEIR DEAD

Part of the great pain of grief is that sense of the enormous gulf that separates the living from the dead. Often, in the case of a sudden death, the bereaved will say, 'He was there one minute, and the next he was gone.' And this will be said not only with great sorrow but also with great puzzlement, because there is something so very mysterious in all this. It is something to do with the mystery of people going somewhere, yet without their bodies. It is somehow 'spooky' and altogether rather frightening, and in a way one wonders whether they are going to still be friendly in their new condition and place. 'But where are they?' is an often asked question. C. S. Lewis expresses this so well in *A Grief Observed*, where he asks this question about his recently deceased wife, whom he refers to as 'H':

'Where is she now?' That is, in what place is she at the

present time? But if H is not a body – and the body I loved is certainly not she – she is in no place at all. And the 'present time' is a date or point in our time series. It is as if she were on a journey without me and I said, looking at my watch, 'I wonder is she at Euston now?' But unless she is proceeding at sixty seconds a minute along this same time line that all we living people travel by, what does 'now' mean?[1]

There is a sense in which activity in the next world will always be a puzzle to us, and thank goodness for that or it would be a great disappointment. But this sense of distance is not helped by us taking a rigorous separatist view of the dead. If a man has loved his wife for forty-five years and one day she is suddenly in a different world, he does not stop loving her. Indeed for the believer it would be a sign of weak faith to stop loving her, because that would imply that she no longer existed, which, in Christ, she does. But how does he show his love for her? Obviously he can no longer cuddle her, bring her cups of tea, talk to her, listen to her, walk with her and do all the thousands of things that communicated love in this world. He has to find a new language of love that can communicate to her world.

And this of course is the great attraction of spiritualism. There is no doubt that spiritualism meets this need, though through totally unchristian and deceptive means. But the reason spiritualism has thrived is because the Church has had very little to offer the bereaved. But Christian hope has so much to offer! We are permitted to love our dead, just as the early Christians did – as is revealed in the tomb inscriptions mentioned in chapter 3. It is true we cannot engage in conversation, and we cannot do all the things that meant so much to us here in this world. But there is now part of us in heaven, and we have to use heaven's ways of expressing our love. Prayer for the dead in the sort of ways that we have discussed in this book, is simply a way of expressing our love for the departed.

Adrian Plass writes very movingly about Bishop George Reindorp whose baby daughter, Veronica Jane, died very suddenly at an early age. George Reindorp was enormously comforted by a letter sent to him by a good friend. The letter includes this passage:

> It has been given to me to see our progress to God as a road divided in the middle by a low wall, which we call death. Whatever our age or stage of development, or relationship with other human beings, there is no real change involved in crossing the low wall. We simply continue in a parallel course with those who loved us in our development and relationship. I do not believe that God altered one whit your responsibility or service for your child.
>
> I do believe that she will grow side by side with you, in spirit, as she would have done on earth; and that your prayer and love will serve her development as they would have done on earth. There is nothing static about the other life . . . The companionship which was given you, you still have. The growth to which you look forward will still be yours to watch over and care for.[2]

George Reindorp was given permission to continue to love his daughter in her death, and for him this has been a source of great healing.

MAKING SENSE OF POST-DEATH MEETINGS

It may have come as a surprise to some readers to learn that post-death meetings, where the recently departed makes a sort of return trip to speak to the living are not uncommon. Here are three examples, one from a book I read a few years ago, and two from my own pastoral contacts (whose names I have changed).

Matthew.   In 1987 Bob Jackson wrote his very moving account of the death of his son Matthew and the subsequent journey of grief that he, his wife Christine, and their daughter Ruth had to take. Matthew was a lively 10-year-old boy who died from a fall while the family were holidaying in Austria. Matthew's older sister, Ruth, was also involved in the accident and had to spend some time in hospital recovering. It was during her early days in hospital that she had this experience:

> When Ruth awoke about an hour later her face had miraculously changed and cleared. She looked serene and was smiling.
>
> 'God and Matthew have spoken to me,' she said to Christine who was with her. 'It wasn't a dream, it was much more than that. They were real and they were outside me. God held my hand tight. I could really feel it. Matthew said to me, "You are safe and I am safe, so why worry?" ' 'And what did God say to you, my love?' Christine asked. 'He said, "I love Matthew even more than you do, and I want him with me now." '

Ruth was to know many ups and downs in her adjustment to bereavement, but that encounter was her turning point. A few pages further on in the book Bob Jackson writes:

> Christine's father cried over Matthew each morning for several days until he heard what seemed to be his voice simply saying, 'Don't cry Poppa'.
>
> What are we to make of these things? Perhaps Matthew was allowed to help us in our time of need.[3]

Brian.   Brian is a friend and a member of a church I belonged to. His wife came regularly to church, but Brian only occasionally. In the winter of 1988, his father became very ill and died after Christmas. Brian went over to the family home in Wales for his father's last days, and he was with him when he died.

Soon after his father had breathed his last breath, Brian went downstairs and sat in the familiar chair in the familiar room, but being terribly conscious of the absence of his dad, whom he loved. It was in these moments of quiet, on his own, that he suddenly became aware of the presence of his father. It was more than that experience commonly felt in the early stages of bereavement. It was like a visit, and his father spoke to him and reassured him. For Brian it was a life-changing experience. Not only did it provide him with a profound sense of comfort, but it also convinced him of the reality of the afterlife and the existence of God. He came to see me a few days after this experience and since then his faith has been very important to him.

Mary.   Mary lost her mother shortly before Christmas 1989. In the new year she wrote to me and told me of this experience. Although her mother had been unwell, her death was unexpected and Mary was taken into a deep grief. But in her letter she writes of how she was comforted:

> However, on the next day, as I walked from room to room I found myself looking for someone, or looking to see what this person was doing. Then later I understood. I was upstairs sorting clothes when I suddenly felt love burning into me and something in me recognised my mother – not as she had been in the last few months, but as she was when I was very young. It was someone I had forgotten. She felt young – and free. The next morning – just fleetingly really – I experienced another feeling of freedom and gladness about being free of responsibility. Afterwards I wondered why I hadn't said various things to her, but then I realised none of this happened in my brain. I shall treasure the memory of the love she gave to me at that moment. It was quite in character for my mum. She would have thought that she hadn't thanked me for the last few months and that she hadn't said she loved

me – neither of which I would have expected but which nonetheless she would have wished to have said. Neither would she have wanted me to worry about her, hence the statement of how she was. It certainly made the funeral much easier and I really felt that the coffin had nothing in it that mattered any more.

These are three experiences of different people and there are thousands more who would testify to similar experiences. A few years ago I would have questioned their theology and would have felt distinctly uncomfortable with them. Now, I feel I understand a little more clearly what is happening. The wall is lower than I thought, and such is the greatness of the Lord's compassion and love for us, that he will permit his saints to have these post-death meetings. As usual, some discernment is needed, as clearly some people who claim to have such meetings are experiencing more of an hallucination than an actual meeting. The test is the fruit of such a meeting. If a person is moved on in the process of bereavement and their walk with the Lord becomes deeper as a result, I am inclined to believe the experiences as not only genuine, but also willed by God.

INNER HEALING

Inner healing is now a regular part of many churches' healing ministry, and those who are involved in inner healing will know that many people suffer because of their relationship with close family or friends who have died. The death of that friend or relative does not remove the hurt of a relationship that needed healing. For example, a son who for many years has been unforgiving towards his mother has, while his mother is alive, a chance to offer her forgiveness and seek reconciliation. There is always the hope for healing. But what happens when she has died? I have taken many a funeral where there is a bad atmosphere in the service because of unresolved family hurts and conflicts. The problem is, that once the relative has died, there is apparently no hope for reconciliation.

From time to time I have counselled those who are holding within them powerful feelings of hurt and unforgiveness towards a relative who has died, sometimes many years ago. What do they do with this? A number of us are used to working with a counselling therapy known as 'gestalt'. When appropriate in a bereavement situation, we actually get the person to imagine that the deceased relative is sitting in a chair and the person addresses them and speaks out all that they are feeling. This is a completing work, doing that which the person has been longing to do for some time, to work out of their system the bad feelings that have been in them and to speak out their hitherto unexpressed good feelings. I have seen this type of counselling and inner healing to be tremendously powerful.

You could take this process just one stage further. Take the above example again. The son has these unresolved feelings within him about his deceased mother. He wants to forgive her and get rid of the burden of guilt and the feelings of hurt within him. The gestalt work may well help him, and he could also be encouraged to speak out his forgiveness to his mother in her world beyond the grave. If we are right in believing that the wall is not quite so high as we thought, this spoken act of forgiveness will be heard in paradise and the son will have a powerful experience of having spoken out his forgiveness and a knowledge that his mother has heard. This would most appropriately be done in a prayer time, and the counsellor would then want to bring the good news of forgiveness and healing to the son.

As we have seen in chapter 5, some inner hurt may well be due to the active presence of a departed soul interfering in a person's life. In our inner healing ministry therefore we will want to be open to this dimension and minister to it accordingly.

THE AUTHORITY OF THE CHURCH OVER THE DEAD

The gospels frequently emphasise the authority of Jesus. In the first chapter of Mark's gospel we hear of the crowds being amazed by Jesus because he taught with an authority that the scribes and teachers of the law did not have (Mark 1:22). This comment by Mark is immediately followed by the incident of the demonised man who comes into the synagogue, and Jesus deals with him with consummate authority (v. 25). The authority of Jesus is seen in his words and his deeds. It is emphatic and definite, and he asserts his authority over Satan, who is 'the prince of this world'.

It is therefore not surprising that this authority extends to death and the world of the dead. It is with this authority that he calls back Lazarus from the world of the dead. His voice, used in this world, is heard by the discarnate spirit of Lazarus who is somewhere in the next. Because Jesus' authority reaches beyond the grave, the spirit of Lazarus has to obey and he returns to his body and he is raised back to life. Jesus hands this authority on to his disciples, and therefore in the Acts of the Apostles we find the disciples operating in the power of the Spirit and exercising this authority (in the name of Jesus) over sickness (Acts 9:32–5), nature (Acts 16:25–28), demons (Acts 16:16–18) and death (Acts 9:36–43).

Peter was present when Jesus raised Lazarus and, having learned from Jesus, he is given his turn at doing something similar (Acts 9:36–43). He is called to the home of Tabitha who has died. Interestingly, he is asked to come 'quickly' to the dead Tabitha, probably reflecting the Jewish idea that the spirit remained close to the body only a short while after the death. Their expectation presumably was that, if Peter came in time, the discarnate spirit would still be near enough to hear and respond to Peter. It all speaks of remarkable faith and confidence in the power and authority that they saw in Peter.

When Peter arrives he sends the others out of the room (perhaps he learned this from the raising of Jairus' daughter), and he falls to his knees in prayer. I wonder what he prayed in those moments, kneeling beside the body of Tabitha. My guess is that he was spending time listening to God, discerning whether it was God's will for her spirit to be returned to her body. Having discerned that this was what the Father willed, he works with it and with a word of command he says, 'Tabitha get up,' and she opens her eyes and is clearly back alive again.

We are hearing nowadays a number of accounts of people being brought back from death. I was recently at a conference in London where there was present a man who had been working in a village in South Africa and was used by God to call a woman back to life. I did not meet this man, but I met a close friend of his who verified this story. It takes a lot of discernment to know whether or not it is appropriate to pray in this way (not to say a fair bit of courage!). In his book, *Power Healing*, John Wimber has an interesting section on death. In a discussion on death, he says that Christians need to discern the right time for death (Eccles. 3:2). He illustrates this by writing about an occasion when he was called to a hospital to pray for a baby who was critically ill. He writes:

> When I entered the baby's room, I sensed death, so I quietly said, 'Death get out of here.' It left and the whole atmosphere in the room changed, as though weight were lifted. Then I went over and began praying for the girl . . . Within twenty minutes she improved greatly; several days later she was released completely healed.[4]

On arrival at this hospital room, John Wimber clearly discerned that this was not the time for death and accordingly took authority over it.

We should also note a rather disturbing incident in Acts where death actually occurs as a result of the authority of the apostles (Acts 5:1–11). However we understand this rather strange story of Ananias and Saphira, it is clear that the Church is given authority that extends to death itself.

The Church is therefore clearly given authority to operate in the name of Jesus who is the Resurrection and the Life, and this extends to the realm of death. What does this mean for us? There are two pastoral implications:

Ministry to the dying
This is obviously a highly delicate and sensitive area, and uncaring and thoughtless ministry here can be cruel in the extreme. But accepting this, any ministry to the dying will include a responsibility to listen to God to discern whether the time is right for death. It might just be that the time is not right for death to take place, and this would be the occasion for the Church to rise up in prayer and rebuke death and pray for recovery. However, if it is discerned that now is the appropriate time for death to take place, then again the Church can gather around, not to pray for recovery, but to take its authority and entrust the dying to God and to send them on their way. Jesus entrusted his spirit to God at his death and, according to the same principle, we also release the spirit from this world to travel to the next. The useful booklet, *Ministry to the Sick*, includes some helpful prayers for the dying and commendation of the recently departed.[5]

The funeral service
In my early days of taking funerals it used to strike me as slightly odd that I never directly addressed the deceased. We all talked about him and referred to him, but in a way we tried to pretend that the coffin was not there. The funeral service is often seen as a farewell to the departed, only the departed is not actually part of it. We deal with the body, but we are not

sure what we are doing with the spirit. If we acknowledge that we have been given, in Christ, authority over the dead, then we will have a 'higher view' of what takes place at a funeral. This service has, I believe, a very important role in actually committing the departed to God. In committing the departed to God, we are not assuming that his or her destiny is paradise. We are committing them to God for him to determine where they should go. By doing this we are making it clear that this world is no longer their home.

I make use of a prayer (see the next chapter) which makes clear that I am committing the deceased to God, telling them to leave this world and go on to the next. In this way, I feel I am taking up my authority appropriate for the occasion, and I am making sure that there is no danger of the spirit remaining in this world, causing distress through ghost phenomena. In this way I am ministering to the departing spirit, not to the congregation. What always has to be born in mind of course is that, in a folk religion culture, language of this sort may well encourage their belief in universalism. Ideally therefore there will need to be included in the service some reference to judgement and our accountability before God. It is not an easy path to tread!

Remembering and Releasing

The acts of remembering and releasing are fundamental to our faith. The act of worship that Jesus instituted with his disciples on the night of his betrayal is an act of remembrance. There was nothing strange for the Jew in being told to remember something significant. All their lives, the disciples had been at religious family meals where remembering the great saving acts of God was at the heart of the event. And so, at the last supper, Jesus offers the bread and the wine as symbols of his body and blood and tells the disciples to 'do this in remembrance of me'.

Releasing is also very important in our faith. Jesus spoke to Peter, the man who was going to lead the infant church, telling him, 'Whatever you bind on earth will be bound in heaven, and whatever you loose on earth will be loosed in heaven' (Matt. 16:19). When he appeared to his disciples in the upper room following his death and resurrection, he breathes on them the Holy Spirit and speaks to his disciples about releasing people from their sins (John 20:23). Jesus gives his Church the authority and the power to be involved in a ministry of releasing people from chains that bind them.

This chapter offers some prayers that can be used in certain situations. Some are to do with releasing the dead, and some with remembering them. There is nothing particularly sacrosanct about any of the prayers, and most readers of this book will probably want to adapt them and personalise them in appropriate ways. We don't claim any particular literary merit

for the ones we wrote – they are simply here to give you an
idea of what you can do.

FOR THE DYING

Into Thy merciful hands, O Lord,
we commend the soul of this Thy servant
now departed from the body.
Acknowledge, we meekly beseech Thee,
a work of Thine own hands,
a sheep of Thine own fold,
a lamb of Thine own flock,
a sinner of Thine own redeeming.
Receive him into the blessed arms of Thine unspeakable
    mercy,
into the sacred rest of everlasting peace,
and into the glorious estate of thy chosen saints in heaven.
                        (Bishop Cosin, 1160–1174)

Remember your servant, O Lord,
according to the favour that you bear unto your people
and grant that, increasing in knowledge and love of you,
he may go from strength to strength
and attain to the fullness of joy in your heavenly kingdom,
who lives and reigns in you and the Holy Spirit
now and forever.   Amen.
                (Liturgy of the Episcopal Church of Scotland)

MAKING USE OF ALL SOULS DAY

It is the custom in many churches to send letters to all those
who have been bereaved during the past year to invite them
to come to an All Souls service where their lost loved one will

be remembered. This has all sorts of pastoral and evangelistic benefits, as many of the bereaved will make their way back into church for the first time since the funeral. The point of a service like this will be to remember the deceased before God, in a way that affirms the bereaved's love for them. Permission is given for weeping and the feelings of loss, and the house of God is a safe place for the offering of grief and sorrow. But it is also the occasion for releasing. There will be the releasing of memories of the funeral, and a further releasing of the deceased into death.

The following is an example of a prayer that might be used on an occasion like this:

Gracious Father
At this festival time we rejoice together in the glorious hope
    of resurrection.
We thank you for all who have gone before us
and we remember today those whom we have lost during
    this past year.
We offer you now our love for them
    our memories of them
    all the joys and the sorrows that we shared
    and the grief of recent days.
Give us we pray further strength to face the future and the
    assurance of life eternal.   Amen.

FAMILY PRAYERS

Most families have had an experience of bereavement. In the case of a family where a beloved relative has died in Christ, there may well be something very right and therapeutic about remembering them on the anniversary of their death, as the early Christians were accustomed to doing. For example, where a grandmother has died, and it is known she died putting her trust in God, the family may want to have a short service on the anniversary of her death. Readings can be chosen from 1 Corinthians 15 and other suitable passages, maybe the passage which was used at her funeral. Hymns and songs could be sung which speak of God's comfort and the promise of heaven. The family could make use of symbols, such as candles, flowers, or other signs of resurrection. Then there might be prayers for grandmother. For example,

Lord Jesus,
You are the Resurrection and the Life.
We thank you today for the life of N—
and for all that she meant to us in her life here on earth.
We now remember her
and pray for her that she would know of our love
and would be enjoying all the joys of heaven.
Help us to follow you as she did.
And we rejoice in the hope that one day
we shall walk with her in paradise.   Amen.

PRAYERS OF GOODBYE AT A FUNERAL

As mentioned in the last chapter, the funeral is a very crucial time, both for committing the departed soul to God, and also for saying our farewells. The following is a prayer that could be used at a funeral to help the mourners express what may be going on inside of them.

Loving Father,
If only I had known that N— was going to die so soon.
There were some personal words I would have shared with
    him and some things we had yet to do together.
But I missed the opportunity.

Yet Lord, I do rejoice that you are the God of the living
     and of the dead,
Therefore in your presence I share with N— my unsaid
     words and my unfulfilled deeds.
N—, through Jesus Christ, I speak my words and offer the
     things I would have done for you.

(In a time of silence share your own thoughts with N—)

Father, I thank you for this opportunity to share my heart
     with N— through Jesus Christ your Son.
I now say farewell and release N— to you.
Keep him in the knowledge of your love;
Bring him joy and peace and the assurance of our love for
     him,
Through Jesus Christ, the Resurrection and the
     Life.   Amen.

Some people may like to use the prayer Newman uses in
'The Dream of Gerontius', where those who represent the
Church on Earth commend the departing Gerontius to God.
In 'Ministry to the Sick', the words have been updated and the
prayer reads:

Go forth upon your journey from this world, O Christian
     soul.
In the name of God the Father almighty who created you;
in the name of Jesus Christ who suffered death for you;
in the name of the Holy Spirit, who strengthens you;
in communion with the blessed saints,
and aided by angels and archangels,
     and all the armies of the heavenly host.
May your portion this day be in peace,
     and your dwelling the heavenly Jerusalem.   Amen.[1]

Where the faith of the deceased is not known, I use a more
general prayer:

> Go forth from this world, O soul,
> to that place appointed you by God;
> In the name of the Father who created you,
> and in the name of Jesus Christ who died for you,
> and in the name of the Holy Spirit who gives life to the
>   people of God.
> May the light of God go with you as you journey from this
>   world,
> and may you rest in peace.   Amen.

MISCARRIED PREGNANCY AND STILLBIRTH

At whatever stage the child is lost, an appropriate time of
entrusting the child to God will be of great help to the parents
in the grief process, and will ensure that the life of the child is
entrusted to God. There will be times when the sex of the child
will not be known, though very often the mother has an
intuition about this. Clearly these are highly sensitive occasions,
and great tenderness is needed. The parent will usually know
if they want to name their child. It is sometimes the case that
either you or the parent hear the Lord speaking a name to you,
which makes this service very special.

> Dear Father, we are hurting because the baby we were
>   looking forward to so much has been lost.
> We feel empty and numb and deprived of this precious life.
> Part of us is still looking for her, and search as we might
>   we cannot find her.
> Yet Lord, we know that she is safe with you because you
>   love and cherish every life.

You said, 'Let the little children come to me,' and so we
bring our little daughter to you.

We want her to have the name N—.

Let N— know that she has parents who love her and long
to meet with her again in the garden of paradise when
our family will be truly complete.

We entrust N— to you and ask that she may grow in grace
and in the knowledge of our Lord Jesus Christ. Amen.

or

Almighty and Heavenly Father,

we thank you that we are all created in your image and
share your likeness.

We bring before you our child who was not able to be born
into this life.

In faith we name her N—, and commend her to your
keeping.

We rejoice that she is going to be brought up by Jesus
together with the angels who worship you.

We look forward to that time when we shall all be together
at the coming of our Lord Jesus Christ. Amen.

PRAYERS FOR ABORTED LIVES

In our experience many parents, particularly mothers, find a
need for prayer and committal to God of a life they lost through
abortion. It is difficult to find a prayer to suit everyone, because
it is always going to be such a personal experience. In this
prayer we are assuming that the parent is wanting to express
sorrow and is seeking forgiveness. It is a prayer of releasing
the soul of the child, and of releasing the parent from guilt.

Most gracious Father, I ask your forgiveness for my sins

and especially I am sorry that the life of my child was taken through abortion.

I am grateful, Lord, that you do know all about the pressures, the difficulties and the problems that caused me to take that decision.

Whatever my reasons, Lord, I am truly sorry for the taking of this life.

I ask forgiveness from you and from my child who has died.

I take this opportunity to acknowledge before God that I do have a child and recognise him as my own.

Please receive this child into your care, and assure him of my love.

In faith I name him N— and I look forward to that day when, through faith in Christ Jesus, we may be reunited in paradise.   Amen.

PRAYERS FOR FORGOTTEN CHILDREN

In our experience it is quite common to find that parents can become acutely aware of the child they lost through miscarriage or abortion, many years after the event. Grief which has been trapped inside for a long time finds its way to the surface and breaks out, and the parent recognises the existence of another member of their family. At an appropriate time during the counselling process one of the following prayers may be helpful:

Dear Lord Jesus,

you were always glad to be in the company of children and taught us that we must be like them to be in the kingdom of heaven.

As parents, we now realise that we have more children in our family that we first accepted.

The child who *was* lost through miscarriage *is* also ours.

We are sorry that we have forgotten and ignored him and
  we ask his forgiveness and yours.
It helps us to know that no child is lost to you.
Therefore, in faith, we now name our child N— and ask
  you to heal him of any shock or hurt that he has carried
  as a result of the way he died.
Heal the hurt between us, and join us now as one family.
Thank you, Jesus, that you died and rose for our child as
  well as for us, and so we trust that through the coming
  of your kingdom in glory, we shall see him and be
  restored to each other.   Amen.

Loving Father,
we pray for any children today who were miscarried or
  aborted.
We ask you to heal their scars and draw them close to you
  where they will always abide in your love and healing.
Set them free from any shock or hurt that may be preventing
  them from being fully at peace in your Kingdom, so that
  they may joyfully dwell with you in Paradise.
Through Jesus Christ our Lord, Amen.

PRAYERS FOR THE UNQUIET DEAD

We offer here two prayers for use in situations where there is
a member of the family who has died and is still trapped in this
world.

Both prayers ask God to take the soul who has died away
from this world to the next. We do recognise that in some cases
the eternal destiny of the soul will not be known. In the prayer
we express our hope that the destiny is heaven, but we leave
the judgement to God. These prayers are ones which are
requests to God. Should you want to use a prayer that involves

a direct command to the deceased to leave this world, then you could use one of the funeral prayers above.

> Dear Father,
> In seeking your healing for our home and family, we have learned of the damage done to (by) N— who is our relative.
> We pray in the name of Jesus that you will now remind her of the victory of the cross of your Son Jesus Christ, who died that we might be free from sin and be healed.
> We pray that whatever the sin or problem that has tied her to us will be healed now.
> In the name of Jesus we cut ourselves free and entrust her soul to you.
> Bring her your peace and mercy, and we express before you our hope that she will enter your kingdom and be kept safe until the day when Christ comes again as Saviour and Mighty Conqueror.   Amen.

The following prayer is useful where a particular problem which is besetting a member of the family is seen to be similar to one of a departed family ancestor (e.g. alcoholism, depression, etc.). In this prayer we break any unnatural tie, and say a prayer of release for the ancestor in case that spirit is still having an effect on the living.

> Heavenly Father,
> We have learned that the need we see in N— (*the afflicted family member*), is the same as that of our departed ancestor A—.
> In Jesus' name we cut N— completely free from any influence of A—.
> By your blood shed on the cross have mercy on this family.
> Deliver us from the sins of our forefathers and remove any harmful influence from our family.

We commit to you the soul of A— and ask that you would
  now receive him to yourself.
We ask this in the name of Jesus our Lord who is the
  Resurrection and the Life.   Amen.

BREAKING BONDAGES OVER GENERATIONS

Where there is a clear sense of a bondage which may have its
origins and influence back one or more generations, the following type of prayer will bring a great release. The prayer is in
three parts: the first proclaims the liberating work of Christ and
expresses the situation before God; the second is a deliverance
prayer which sets free the afflicted; the third is a prayer of
healing. Because this is a deliverance prayer it will be essential
to have someone present who is experienced in this type of
ministry.

We thank you, heavenly Father, that through the death and
  resurrection of your Son, Jesus Christ, you have
  conquered all the powers of darkness and set the captives
  free.
In the name of Jesus Christ we now stand against the
  unclean spirits which have had their influence down
  through the ages and are now holding N— in bondage.
In the name of Jesus we say to these spirits:
'We break your power over this family and command you
  to get out.
We forbid you to have any more hold over N— and deny
  you all access to her, and we proclaim that the blood of
  Jesus Christ was shed for N— and all her family, bringing
  healing and cleansing from sin.
Go from this family to that place appointed you by God
  and we forbid you to return.
In the name of Jesus Christ who is Lord of all life.   Amen.

You may find you need to continue this stage further, repeating this prayer or using others, until you are satisfied that the deliverance is complete.

> We thank you, Father, that you have broken this bondage
>   and have brought freedom and deliverance to N—.
> Now strengthen and heal him.
> Free him to walk in newness of life, that he may grow daily
>   in the power of your Holy Spirit, through Jesus Christ
>   our Lord.   Amen.

Conclusion

> May the Lord do so to me and more also if even death parts me from you. (Ruth 1:17, RSV)
> The Lord bless him . . . He has not stopped showing his kindness to the living and the dead. (Ruth 2:20)

The subject for heated debate on a television programme 'Friday Night Live'[1] was that of death and survival beyond the grave and whether there were any legitimate means to maintain a relationship with the dead. Various mediums extolled the virtues of their craft whilst the Christian belief in the death, resurrection and lordship of Jesus Christ was firmly represented by the Revd Graham Dow of Holy Trinity Church in Coventry. The programme was in response to a film entitled *Ghost*. Basically the story line is that of a young man who is suddenly killed and who, because of the shock and impact of his own death, is unable to leave his familiar surroundings to go to heaven. He finds that he cannot tell his fiancée how much he loves her although he is present with her as she tries to come to terms with the tragedy. What was significant about this film was that it attracted millions of young people to watch it and has consequently become a box-office success. Whilst not wishing to endorse the spiritualism portrayed in the film, for reasons already stated in this book, there are some factors which the film underlines which are of real concern for Christians. First, the subject is of sufficient importance to draw large numbers of young people who, it may be reasonable to assume, have not lost a loved one but for whom survival beyond this life is important. Secondly, the central message of the film is the idea that both the living and the dead do not stop loving and caring about each other after death has occurred.

The whole purpose of this book is to affirm that because Jesus is Lord of the living and the dead and holds the key to a salvation which extends beyond this present world, that it is only in him that these concerns find healing and fulfilment. The grief process, although it follows a defined pattern, is nonetheless a very personal journey for each person.

For many, grief comes as a rude awakening as they realise that a miscarriage or an abortion involves a real life. Bernadette Thompson, a care assistant with mentally handicapped adults in Halifax, has shared how she was in a self-destructive state following an abortion. She says, 'I fooled myself into thinking it was just a mass of cells . . . it was not until years after the abortion that I was able to face up to what I had done and then realise what I was suffering from was grief. I was mourning my lost baby.'[2] She goes on to explain how the guilt in her destroyed her two marriages and that she was unable to find peace until she received some Christian counselling. Although painful at first, for Bernadette it came as a healing experience to realise that she was indeed grieving for a lost life. For through the resurrected Christ we can proclaim that although some lives have been lost to us, they have not been lost to God, and that at the final resurrection we shall all be together at the coming of Christ (see 1 Thess. 4:15–18).

For others it is not a forgotten life which causes problems with the grief process but the fact that they have not been able to let go of the deceased. Whether this is a case of projecting hurt feelings or that somehow the dead have been prevented from completing their journey, it is good to know that through Jesus Christ there can be a healing and a letting-go of the departed. It is perhaps important at this stage to suggest that not only the living but also the departed experience bereavement. Sheldon Venauken was comforted by this thought when he shared his feelings of loss with his friend and mentor, C. S. Lewis.

> He [C. S. Lewis] was thoughtful about the idea of the dead undergoing bereavement..one of us suggested that if the dead do stay with us for a time, it might be allowed partly so that we may hold on to something of their reality.[3]

He goes on to share how Lewis stated that in our journey towards the Eternal Being there was a necessary element of bereavement and that this matched Jesus' words when he said, 'It is expedient that I go away.'[4] Venauken endorses the need to hold on to the departed but says that eventually God brings us to the 'Christ place' where we allow them to go away, having realised that, because we have been shaped by those we love, we hold a deposit of their lives within us.

A final area we have considered are the unquiet dead, commonly called 'ghosts'. These are brought to our attention either by the presence of unexplained phenomena such as noises, tappings, the opening and closing of doors even when locked, or by sightings of the dead who seem preoccupied or distressed. Such reportings do need careful checking in order to eliminate any subjective projecting of the individual's own concerns and worries. If there has been a resorting to spiritualism, this needs to be repented of and renounced in the name of the Lord Jesus. However, if after such precautions the phenomenon does seem to involve some form of unquiet death, then what is needed is the healing of the death and not the ministry of exorcism. Duncan and Joyce Wainwright have recently published a pamphlet entitled *The Great Release*, which details an account concerning the appearance of a maid in one of the rooms of a Christian conference centre in the Midlands. Various prayers of deliverance had been offered by a former minister but to no avail. However, Duncan and Joyce, along with another minister and a lady parish worker, conducted a form of the Lord's

Supper in this room in May 1990. They felt that they were declaring to this maid that the Lord Jesus had died for her sins and that, because of this, they wished to point out that whatever her personal sorrow or sins these were all laid on Jesus. It must be said that such prayers are not a claim to offer salvation after death but to show the unquiet dead that Jesus is Lord of their times and, in so doing, release the departed from this world into the next. As a consequence of their prayers and recognition of the deceased, the Wainwrights reported that all the disturbing events ceased from the building and that there were no further sightings of the maid; a calmness and a lightness had returned to the centre.

In this book we have tried to underline that a Christian response to these 'unquiet deaths' is not to dismiss them as so much speculation but to bring the lives and deaths concerned to Jesus, who by nature of his eternal being has access to all life both in this world and the next. Jesus is the true healing presence and is uniquely qualified to bring a proper fulfilment to our grief. As in the circumstances of Martha and Mary, he comes to our unresolved death, shares our feelings and, at the same time, says that he is the resurrection and the life. Jesus commanded that the stone which blocked Lazarus's exit from the tomb be removed. In a similar way, he enables us to speak to the mountains which block our way forward in life and see them removed.[5] This is not a pretext for spiritualism but rather an encouragement to bring to Jesus either the forgotten deaths of our miscarried children or the unquiet deaths which exert undue influence over our lives.

In concluding this book we offer some thoughts which may enable us to have a more fulfilling attitude toward those whom we love but, for the moment, see no longer. First of all, we see that it is perfectly acceptable to love our dead. Consequently we need to be sensitive to people undergoing bereavement and not hurry them through the experience. The time for full letting go must be approached without undue pressure or strain. Secondly, we need to be open to the fact that death does not mean that we cease to be, or that we are incapable of still growing. Therefore those miscarried or aborted lives have a future life in the presence of Jesus. The fact that such lives are growing up in the presence of Jesus offers us an opportunity to ask for forgiveness both from God and from the child itself. Bernadette Thompson said that her life really began to find healing and peace only when she asked the child whom she had aborted for forgiveness for what she had done.[6] Thirdly we have noted that sometimes the illnesses and issues which dominated the lives of our departed relatives can become our troubles too. However, through the power of Jesus Christ, we can bring to God the sins of our forefathers and find healing and release for ourselves. Finally, we have underlined the importance of the Eucharist as a context for requiem healing. It is this sacrament which speaks most powerfully about the death and resurrection of our Lord Jesus. It is only Jesus' death which can speak healing to the death with which we may be dealing. His death tells us that he can go down into all our unquiet deaths and say 'Peace! Be still!' The resurrection of Christ from the dead proclaims that death no longer has the last word. Similarly, the deaths which have been holding us so powerfully have to yield their power up to Christ who will set us free.

Christ has died, but now he is risen and therefore death shall no longer have dominion over us.

Death is swallowed up in victory.
O death, where is thy victory?
O death, where is thy sting? . . .
But thanks be to God, who gives us the victory through our
Lord Jesus Christ. (1 Cor. 15:54–5, 57, RSV)

CHRIST HAS DIED!   **CHRIST IS RISEN!**

CHRIST WILL COME AGAIN!

Notes

INTRODUCTION

1. Kenneth McAll, *Healing the Family Tree* (Sheldon Press, 1989), p. 3.
2. Michael Mitton, *The Quick and the Dead* (Grove Books, Pastoral Series, 1987).

CHAPTER 1: FEELINGS FOR THE DEAD

1. Quoted by Judith Cook in *An Accident Waiting to Happen* (Unwin Paperbacks, 1989), p. 6.
2. Quoted by Jim Graham in *Dying to Live* (Marshall, 1984), pp. 150–1.
3. Elisabeth Kübler-Ross, *On Death and Dying* (Tavistock Publications, 1973).
4. Quoted in an article, 'Obituaries and Pastoral Care', *Journal of Pastoral Studies*, 98 (1989), p. 28.
5. Maxine Negri, 'Age Old Problems of the New Age Movement', *Humanist* (March-April 1988), pp. 23–4.
6. Raymond A. Moody Jr, *Life After Life* (Mockingbird, Covington GA, 1975). See also *Beyond Death's Door* by Maurice Rawlings (Nelson, New York, 1975), which describes how the author's scepticism about Christianity and the need to be personally converted is deeply challenged by the resuscitation stories of his patients.
7. Matthew and Dennis Linn, *Healing the Greatest Hurt* (Paulist Press, 1985), pp. 181–2.

8. Rawlings, op. cit. p. 7.
9. *Church of England Newspaper*, 1 December 1989.
10. Jean Darnell, *Heaven Here I Come* (Lakeland, 1974), pp. 35–44.
11. Duncan Munro, *Sickness Unto Death* (Grove Books, Ethics Series, no. 30), p. 8.
12. Sheila Cassidy, *Sharing the Darkness* (Darton Longman and Todd, 1989), p. 59.
13. Amy Carmichael, *Fragments that Remain*, ed. Bee Trehane (SPCK Triangle, 1987), p. 145. Quoted by permission of the publisher.

CHAPTER 2: MEEETING WITH THE DEAD

1. Matt. 22:32. Paul applies exactly the same description of lordship over the living and the dead to Jesus Christ (Rom. 14:9).
2. The Hebrew term which is translated 'grave', 'hell' or 'pit' in the King James version.
3. Job 10:22; Ps. 88:12, 94:17, 115:17.
4. Isa. 14:9–11; Ezek. 32:17-end.
5. Other Old Testament references to a hope beyond the grave include Ps. 49:15, 83:24; Job 19:25–6.
6. See also Mat 9:24; 27:52; John 11:11–12; 1 Cor. 11:30, 15:20, 51.
7. Quoted by William Barclay in *Death and the Life to Come* (Hodder and Stoughton, 1988), p. 29.
8. William Temple, *Readings in St John's Gospel* (Macmillan, 1949), p. 226f.
9. Ibid., p. 227.
10. J. Norval Geldenhuys, *Commentary on the Gospel of Luke* (Marshall, Morgan and Scott, 1971), p. 615.
11. See 2 Cor. 5:8; Phil. 1:23.
12. Exod. 22:18; 2 Chron. 33:6; Isa. 2:6–9; Mic. 5:12; Nah. 3:4.
13. Alexander Maclaren, *Exposition of Holy Scripture*, vol. 3, (Hodder and Stoughton, 1905), p. 376.
14. 1 Sam. 16:14, 18:10–11, 21, 25; 19:1, 15, 20, 30–3.
15. *Wilmington's Guide to the Bible*, Tyndale House, Illinois, 1986, p. 107.

16. John J. Davis, 'The Birth of a Kingdom', *Brethren Missionary Herald* (1970), pp. 96–9.

17. J. C. Ryle, *Expository Thoughts on the Gospels* (Charles J. Thynne, 1897), p. 205.

18. Alexander Maclaren, *Exposition of Holy Scripture*, vol. 2: *Matthew* (Hodder and Stoughton, 1905), pp. 347–8.

19. H. A. Ironside, *Commentary on Matthew* (Loiseaux Bros, 1981), pp. 210–1.

20. R. T. France, *Tyndale Commentary on Matthew* (Inter-Varsity Press, 1985), p. 262.

21. Maclaren, *Exposition of Holy Scripture*, vol. 3, p. 546.

22. John H. Hampsch, *Healing Your Family Tree* (Performance Press), 1986.

23. Matthew and Dennis Linn with Sheila Fabricant, *Healing the Greatest Hurt* (Paulist Press, 1985), pp. 42–9.

24. William Barclay, *Daily Study Bible: Hebrews* (St Andrew's Press, 1976), p. 172.

25. Alexander Maclaren, *Exposition of Holy Scripture: Hebrews* (Hodder and Stoughton, 1910), p. 167.

26. Ibid., p. 168.

27. *The Speakers Bible: Hebrews* (Speakers Bible Office, 1931), p. 319.

28. Isa. 24:21–2; 2 Pet. 2:4; Rev. 20:1–7. See also William Barclay, *Daily Study Bible: James, Peter* (St Andrew's Press, 1976), pp. 236f.; also E. C. S. Gibson *The Thirty Nine Articles* (Methuen 1912), pp. 159–65, for a description of the intermediate state of the saints in the Old Testament. The 1553 form of Article III reads:

> As Christ died and was buried for us; so also it is to be believed that he went down into hell. For the body lay in the sepulchre until the resurrection, but his ghost departing from him was with the ghosts that were in prison or in hell and did preach to the same, as the place of St Peter doth testify.

29. *New Bible Dictionary* (Inter-Varsity Press 1970), p. 1212.

30. 1 Pet. 4:6. For the term *pneuma* to describe human personality see 2 Cor. 7:1; Col. 2:5. For human perception, see Mark. 2:8; Luke 1:47; 1 Pet. 3:4.

31. Barclay, *Daily Bible Study: Hebrews*, p. 241.
32. Mentioned by E. C. S. Gibson, op. cit., p. 169.
33. Mentioned by Leon Morris in *Commentary on Corinthians* (Inter-Varsity Press, 1983) p. 218.
34. William Barclay, *Daily Study Bible: Corinthians* (St Andrew's Press, 1975), p. 153.

CHAPTER 3:   PRAYERS, PURGATORY AND PROTESTANTS

1. The Authorised Daily Prayer Book of the United Hebrew Congregation of the British Commonwealth of Nations (Eyre and Spottiswoode, 1962) p. 431.
2. Josephus 'Discourse to the Greeks concerning Hades'.
3. I am indebted here to a pamphlet by Michael Rear entitled *Praying for the Dead* (Church Literature Association), who records these inscriptions. His source is H. P. V. Nunn, *Christian Inscriptions – Texts for Students* (SPCK, 1920).
4. Quoted in Peter Brown's *The Cult of the Saints* (SCM Press, 1981), p. 106. His reference is Jerome, Ep. 103. 13.
5. E. L. Blant, *Les inscriptions Chrétiennes de la Gaule* (Paris Imprémière Imperiale, 1856), 1:240.
6. Clement, *Stromateis*, 7:6.
7. Augustine, *De Civitate Dei*, 21:13, 24.
8. Brother Ramon, *Fulness of Joy* (Marshall Pickering, 1988), p. 205.
9. J. Graham, *Dying to Live* (Marshall, 1984).
10. Jesus uses the term 'asleep' to describe the condition of Jairus's daughter before he raises her (Luke 8:51–6). The girl is seen to be 'asleep' until her spirit returns to her body. The same is true of Lazarus. Jesus says, 'Our friend Lazarus is asleep, but I am going to wake him up' (John 11:11–13). Sleep therefore describes the separation between spirit and body that takes place at death.
11. For a fuller outline of these stages, see my booklet *The Quick and the Dead* (Grove Books, Pastoral Series, no. 32.).
12. Quoted by Alan Wilkinson in *The Church of England and the First World War* (SPCK, 1978), p. 175.
13. Ibid., p. 177.

14. Full text of the prayer is in G. K. A. Bell, *Randall Davidson* (OUP, 1938), p. 828–9.

CHAPTER 4: HURTINGS AND HAUNTINGS

1. Michael Perry (ed.), *Deliverance* (SPCK, 1987), p. 38.
2. Raphael Gasson, *The Challenging Counterfeit* (Logos, 1966), p. 33.
3. Kenneth McAll, *Healing the Haunted* (Darley Anderson, 1989), p. 38.
4. Perry (ed.), op. cit., p. 38–9.
5. J. B. Phillips, *Ring of Truth* (Hodder and Stoughton, 1985), ch. 2.

CHAPTER 5: HEALINGS AND REQUIEMS

1. John Wesley, 'A Second Letter to the Author of *The Enthusiasm of Methodists and Papists Compared*', quoted in E. R. Hardy, 'The Blessed Dead in Anglican Piety', *Sobornost*, vol. 3, no. 2 (1981), pp. 179–91.
2. Whilst being a pioneer for this approach to ministry, Dr McAll is by no means alone. Within the Church of England he has encouraged and shared in the work of Neil Broadbent, who is based in Derby, and also Robert Law, who is the Bishop of Truro's adviser on the ministry of deliverance.
3. From a taped interview at Bignell Wood, Hants, September 1988.
4. Leanne Payne, *The Broken Image* (Crossway Books, Westchester, Ill. 1986).
5. Kenneth McAll, *Healing the Family Tree* (Sheldon Press, 1989), pp. 7–9.
6. Ibid., taped interview.
7. Kenneth McAll, 'The Church's Ministry of Healing and Healing of the Family Tree': a discussion paper, unpublished and undated, p. 4.

8. See e.g.: Luke 10:8–16; John 3:16–17, 5:28–30; Eph. 2:1–7; 2 Thess. 1:5–10; Heb. 9:27, 10:27; 2 Pet. 2:4–9, 3:7.

9. McAll, op. cit., *taped interview*.

10. We should not be too disturbed at the subject of visions itself. This phenomenon is becoming more and more a feature of healing ministry within the experience of spiritual renewal. The term vision is perhaps too sweeping, and so some people prefer to use the term 'a picture from God'. However, Dr McAll would say that his visionary experience is quite substantial and not merely a subjective or inward perception. He refers to the opening of the tombs, mentioned in Matthew's Gospel, as a visualisation similar to his own encounters at requiem Eucharists. This is not convincing, as the account in Matthew 27, itself a product of the death and resurrection of Jesus, is not presented as a vision and contains all the hallmarks of an historic encounter of restored life on the Lazarus scale. Dr McAll and the two associates previously mentioned (note 2) report that they have seen, through visions, a number of the deceased for whom they are praying, attending the requiem Eucharists, sometimes accompanied by angels.

11. Lev. 16:1ff, 26:39–45; Num. 15:22–6; Lam. 5:7.

12. Exod. 20:5, 34:7–9; Num. 14:18–20.

13. Raphael Gasson, *The Challenging Counterfeit* (Logos International, 1968), pp. 13–14.

14. Russ Parker, *The Occult: Deliverance from Evil* (Inter-Varsity Press, 1989).

15. Dr Kurt Koch, *Christian Counselling and Occultism* (Kregel, 1972), p. 307.

16. McAll, op. cit., p. 66.

17. Dennis and Matthew Linn with Sheila Fabricant, *Healing the Greatest Hurt* (Paulist Press, 1985), pp. 54–5.

CHAPTER 6: JESUS THE MODEL FOR REQUIEMS

1. Proper Preface in the First Eucharistic Prayer, Rite A, *The Alternative Service Book* (Clowes/SPCK etc., 1980), p. 131.
   The Sanctus is that part of the Church of England Service which proclaims:

> Holy, holy, holy,
> God of power and might,
> heaven and earth are full of your glory.
> Hosanna in the highest.

2. *Alternative Service Book*, p. 132.

CHAPTER 7: REQUIEM HEALING AND PASTORAL CARE

1. C. S. Lewis, *A Grief Observed* (Faber, 1961), p. 22.
2. A. Plass, *The Growing Up Pains of Adrian Plass* (Marshall, 1986), p. 100.
3. Bob Jackson, *Matthew* (Highland, 1987), pp. 42, 45.
4. John Wimber, *Power Healing* (Hodder, 1986), p. 174.
5. 'Ministry to the Sick', *Authorised Alternative Services 1983*.

CHAPTER 8: REMEMBERING AND RELEASING

1. 'Ministry to the Sick', *Authorised Alternative Services*, p. 39.

CONCLUSION

1. 'Friday Night Live', Central Television, 5 October 1990.
2. *The Independent*, 22 January 1988, p. 16.
3. Sheldon Venauken, *A Severe Mercy* (Hodder, 1970), pp. 226ff.
4. Ibid., p. 232.
5. Matt. 17:20–1; cf. Luke 17:6 where the same instructions are given with regard to uprooting the mulberry bush.
6. *The Independent*, 22 January 1988, p. 16.